# Choosing & Using Gunsmithing Tools and Techniques: Part II

Hands-on instruction for basic and advanced gun work.

ISBN: 1-879-620-51-0

**Please Note:** The information appearing in this publication is presented for educational purposes only. In no case shall the publishers be held responsible for any use readers may choose to make, or not to make, of this information.

The American Gunsmith Library
Volume Six

BASIC AND ADVANCED
FIREARMS MAINTENANCE

# Choosing & Using Gunsmithing Tools and Techniques: Part II

## Hands-on Instruction for Basic and Advanced Gun Work

By the Editors of AMERICAN GUNSMITH Magazine

**AG Media, Inc.
Greenwich, Connecticut 06836**

# Contents

# Section Two: Techniques ...... 105

# Preface

One of the truisms of the gunsmithing business is that the smart gunsmith learns from his own mistakes, but the wise gunsmith learns from the mistakes of others. If we're smart, our most prized gun-repair and gun-modification skills tend to be the knowledge we won by scraping our knuckles with a careless pass of a wood rasp. But if we're wise, we note and avoid such problems before they occur, which means we pay attention to the work of 'smiths who preceded us. By learning from the mistakes of our fellows, we also learn about their solutions for problems as common as preventing hex-head screws from stripping or as esoteric as keeping checkering tools on line.

The sixth and final volume in the *AMERICAN GUNSMITH* Library series, *Choosing & Using Gunsmithing Tools and Techniques: Part II*, passes on hundreds of expert gunsmiths' tips for repairing and upgrading revolvers, bolt-action rifles, pump shotguns, semiauto long guns, pistols, and other firearms. You'll find out the best stock-carving tools, examine how to blue and finish metal for durability and beauty, investigate the nuances of installing front sights, and read about hundreds of other hard-earned nuggets of gunsmithing experience.

We believe this hands-on information, written by professional gunsmiths who've spent years at the bench, can save you money by teaching you how to repair your own guns or the guns of your friends. Also, the material in this book can make you a more proficient shooter by helping you understand how different guns work.

We hope you enjoy reading and learning more about your favorite guns, and the tools and techniques that support them, in *Choosing & Using Gunsmithing Tools and Techniques: Part II.*

—*The Editors of AMERICAN GUNSMITH*

# Section One

# Tools and Toolmaking

# 1.

# Choosing and Using Files: The Selection

*Metalwork can be smoother and better when the proper files are used. Here is a rundown of the major tool choices.*

*By Dennis A. Wood*

An old toolmaker, who had the responsibility of training young upstarts, once told me, "Give me a trainee that knows how to file and I'll teach him the rest." According to this old gentleman, quite a bit of his early apprenticeship involved the proper uses of files, and this old guy used a file like a concert violinist uses a bow.

Gunsmiths, too, have plenty of opportunities to file wood and metal, and using a file properly can speed—or even make possible—your work on internal bolt parts, stocks, and other piecework. For instance, when I'm hard-fitting parts that are purposely made oversize, the proper type and use of a file will make the job go easier. Or when I'm installing so-called drop-in parts for building 1911 auto pistols, more often than not I find myself reaching for a file to give the parts a few swipes so they will actually drop in.

Filing is one of those tasks you develop a feel for, a learn-by-doing process. But first, let's talk about the kinds of files that gunsmiths regularly employ.

## Talking The Talk

Files are normally classified according to their shape or cross-cut section and according to the pitch or spacing of their teeth and the nature of the cut. The broad terms used to describe file characteristics are cross-section and outline.

A file's cross section may be triangular, quadrangular, circular, or some special shape. The outline of its contour may be tapered or blunt.

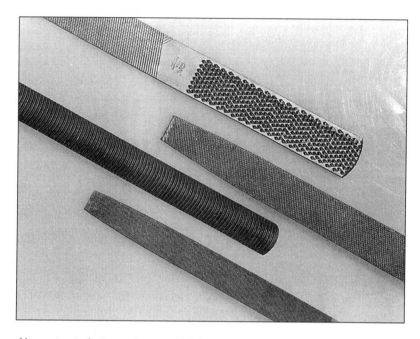

*Above, top to bottom:* A rasp, which is used to remove large amounts of wood; the bastard cut file, which is used primarily for roughing metal work but which will also serve to work wood; the curved tooth file, used for shaping stocks or other wood work; and the second-cut pattern, which is used for metalwork.

In the former the point is reduced in width and/or thickness gradually, usually for one-half to two-thirds of its length. Blunt files' cross sections remain the same from tang to point.

The term "cut" designates the arrangement of teeth, such as single, double, rasp, or curved. The single-cut file has a single series of parallel teeth extending across the face of the file at an angle of 45 to 85 degrees with the axis of the file (see sidebar for definitions). This angle depends upon the form of the file and the nature of the work for which the file is intended. The single cut file is normally used with light pressure to produce a smooth finish.

The double-cut file has a large number of small pointed teeth angling toward the point of the file arranged in two series of diagonal rows that cross each other. For general work, the angle of the first series of rows is from 40 to 45 degrees and the second row from 70 to 80 degrees. For double-cut finishing files, the first series has an angle of about 30 degrees, and the second from 80 to 87 degrees. The second, or upcut, is almost always deeper than the first or overcut. Double-cut files are usually used, along with heavier pressure, for removing material faster and where you can get by with a rougher finish.

The rasp is formed by raising a series of individually rounded teeth from the surface of the file blank and is used with relatively heavy pressure on softer material for faster removal such as roughing out the shape on gun stocks.

The curved-tooth file has teeth that are in the form of parallel arcs extending across the face of the file. The middle portion of each arc is closest to the point or center of the file. Teeth are usually single cut and are relatively coarse.

## Coarseness

Files remove material at different rates; the terms coarse, bastard, second, and smooth are normally used to describe those rates. The coarse and bastard-cut files are used to remove a great deal of material from a job, and the second and smooth cut files are used to finish the more exacting gun work.

You'll often find more use for the second and smooth cut files on metal, and the rougher cut files for stock wood shaping. (Degrees of coarseness are only comparable when files of the same length are compared, as the number of teeth per inch decreases as the length of the file increases.) The coarseness range for curved tooth files is given as standard, fine and smooth. In the case of Swiss pattern files a series of numbers is used to designate coarseness instead of a title; numbers 00, 0, 1, 2, 3, 4, and 6 are the most common, with No. 00 the coarsest and No. 6 the finest. The number 5 is not used because it could be mistaken for an "S" on a smooth-cut file.

## File Classes

There are five main classes of files: mill or saw files, machinist files, curved tooth files, Swiss-pattern files, and rasps.

The first two classes are more commonly referred to as American pattern files. Mill or saw files are used for sharpening mill or circular saws, large cross-cut saws, lathe work, draw filing brass or bronze and for general smooth filing. Cantsaw files have an obtuse isosceles triangular section, a blunt outline, are single cut and are used for sharpening saws having "M" shaped teeth and teeth of less than a 60 degree angle. Crosscut files have a narrow triangular section with the short side rounded, a blunt outline, a single cut and are used to sharpen crosscut saws. Machinist files are used throughout industry where metal must be removed rapidly and where the finish is not that important.

Except for certain instances in the round or half-round configurations,

# File Definitions

**Axis:** The imaginary line extending the entire length of a file equidistant from the faces and edges.

**Back:** The convex side of a file having the same or similar cross-section as in a half-round file.

**Bastard Cut:** A grade of coarseness that falls between coarse and second cut on American pattern files and rasps.

**Blank:** A file in any process of manufacture before the teeth are cut.

**Blunt:** A file whose cross-section dimensions from point to tang remain unchanged.

**Coarse Cut:** The coarsest of all American pattern files and rasps.

**Coarseness:** This term describes the relative number of teeth per length of the file. The coarsest have the fewest number of teeth per unit of length; the smoothest files the most. American pattern files and rasps have four degrees of coarseness; coarse, bastard, second and smooth. Swiss pattern files usually have seven stages of coarseness: 00, 0, 1, 2, 3, 4 and 6 (from coarsest to smoothest). Curved-tooth files have three stages of coarseness; standard, fine and smooth.

**Curved Cut:** File teeth that are made in a curved contour across the file blank.

**Cut:** This term is used to describe the file teeth with respect to coarseness or character. Single, double, rasp, curved or special are used to describe the cut.

**Double Cut:** A file tooth arrangement formed by two series of cuts, namely the overcut followed, at an angle, by the upcut.

**Edge:** The surface joining faces of a file. Some files have teeth on the edges, some don't.

most of these files are double cut.

Flat files have a rectangular section, are tapered in width and thickness, cut on both sides and edges and are used for general utility work. Half-round files have a circular segmental section, are tapered in width and thickness, have their flat side double cut, their rounded side mostly double cut but sometimes single cut and are used to file in concave areas. Hand files are similar to flat files but taper in thickness only. One edge is usually uncut or safe. Knife files have a knife blade shaped section, tapered in width only, double cut and are used by tool and die makers on work having acute angles. General-purpose files have a

**Face:** The widest cutting surface or surfaces that are used for filing. Heel or Shoulder: That portion of a file that abuts the tang.

**Hopped:** This term is used by file makers to describe the spacing between file teeth.

**Length:** The distance from the heel to the point of the file.

**Overcut:** The first series of teeth put on a double cut file.

**Point:** The front end of a file.

**Rasp Cut:** A file tooth arrangement of round-topped teeth, not usually connected. These teeth are formed individually by means of a narrow punch like tool.

**Recut:** A worn out file which has had the teeth re-cut into it after annealing and grinding off of the old teeth. The file is then re-hardened.

**Safe Edge:** An edge on a file that is smooth and without teeth so that it will not cut into the workpiece.

**Second Cut:** A grade of file coarseness between bastard and smooth on American pattern files and rasps.

**Set:** To blunt the sharp edges or corners of file blanks before and after the overcut is made. This is done to prevent weakness or breakage of the teeth along the edges or corners when the file is in use.

**Single Cut:** File tooth arrangement where the file teeth are composed of single unbroken rows of parallel teeth formed by a single series of cuts.

**Smooth Cut:** An American pattern file and rasp cut that is smoother than second cut.

**Tang:** The narrowed end of the file which enters the handle.

**Upcut:** The series of teeth superimposed on the overcut and at an angle to it, such as on a double-cut file.

rectangular section, are tapered and have second cut teeth divided by angular sections which produce short cutting edges. These edges help with stock removal but still leave a smooth finish and are suitable for use on various materials including aluminum, bronze, cast iron and mild steels.

Pillar files are similar to hand files but are thicker and narrower and should be included in every gunsmiths arsenal of files. Because these files are thicker there is less tendency for this type of file to flex. Round files have a circular surface, are tapered, single cut and are generally used to file round openings or convex radii. Three-square files are double cut and have sharp corners as contrasted with taper triangular files, which are single cut and have somewhat rounded corners. These files are normally used for filing accurate internal angles such as those used for dovetail sight bases. Warding files have a rectangular section and taper in width to a narrow point. These files are used for getting into narrow areas.

Wood files are made in the same sections as flat and half round files but with coarser teeth especially suited for rough work on gunstocks. Curved tooth files are made in both rigid and flexible forms. The rigid type has either a tang for a conventional handle or is made with a hole at each end for mounting in a special holder. The flexible type is furnished for use in special holders only. Curved tooth files come in standard, fine and smooth cuts in parallel flat, square, pillar, pillar narrow, half round and shell types.

Swiss pattern files are used by tool and die makers, model makers and delicate instrument parts finishers. These files are made to closer tolerances than the conventional American pattern files although they have similar cross-sections. The points of the Swiss pattern files are smaller, the tapers are longer and they are available in much finer cuts. These files are primarily finishing tools for removing burrs left behind from previous finishing operations, truing up grooves, notches, cleaning out corners and smoothing small parts. For very fine work, round and square handled needle files, available in numerous cross-section shapes in lengths from 4 to 7$^1$/$_4$ inches, are used. ★

# 2.

# Choosing and Using Files: Hands-On Help

*Other than screwdriver bits and punches, files are probably the most useful tools gunsmiths can own. Here's how to get more out of them.*

*By Dennis A. Wood*

Given time and patience, any job performed on a milling machine can probably be done by hand with files. Once properly inletted, a decent stock design can be rasped out of a block of walnut, providing a nesting place for a favorite barreled action. A replacement rabbit ear hammer for that antique shotgun can be fashioned out of a piece of steel. The artisans of bygone times did not have all the intricate wood or metal-shaping equipment available today, yet they managed to turn out beautiful work. When filing, patience and the ability to see the finished job in your mind make the difference between success and failure—along with using proper filing techniques.

You already know some of the techniques involved, but there are some basic file-working ideas that are worth reviewing and some advanced techniques that can make your work go faster and look better.

## Choosing A File

When working on any surface, the most important step is to choose the right file cut, style, and size.

A milling machine (which removes metal, as does a file) has the incremental capacity for downfeed adjustment. If the mill downfeed scale is accurate, the cutter will remove the desired amount of material from the work piece. Not so with files. The operator determines how much material is removed with each pass of the file. This is why selecting the right file-cut type is important.

To get a real-world idea of how much material each file removes, place a flat piece of steel stock, and with a micrometer or vernier, measure

## Power Files

Using rotary files and burr bits in a motor-driven hand tool can add speed to your filing, especially on softer materials such as wood, but they also have application on metal.

A round, coarse burr bit, for instance, removes wood from a gunstock quickly in preparation for a glass bedding job.

Also, the cylinder and tapered carbide burr bits are handy for shaving metal, especially in hard-to-get-at areas. This works well when installing and blending flared magazine-well extensions on 1911s.

Additionally, small carbide ball burr bits are handy to use when a screw slot is butchered up, and you need to get the screw out for replacement. The little ball will cut a good enough slot so that the battered screw can be turned out.

the thickness of it. Place the steel stock in your vise and take ten or so swipes across the top of it with a smooth-cut file. Measure the piece again, and you will soon see that not much material has been removed by the smooth cut file.

Thus, when a project calls for removing $1/32$ inch of material, start

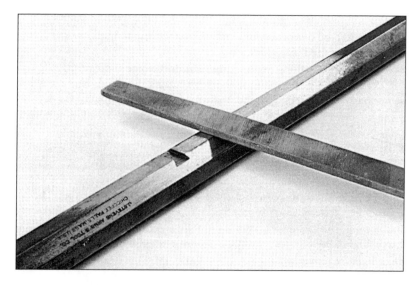

**Above:** *While draw filing, the file teeth are held at 90 degrees to the bore line, and the file is pushed forward and back.*

the job with one of the coarser files, such as the bastard cut. Work the surface down with the coarse file until there is about 0.010-inch of remaining material, then finish up with one of the smoother cuts.

Shaping gun stock wood normally calls for coarser files, but this is not to say the finer files do not have a place in working wood. For example, when forming a beaded cheekpiece, it's mighty hard to beat a smooth-cut file to get the definition of a sharp 90-degree shoulder.

Most often, roughing out a stock blank requires using raised tooth rasps in round and half-round shapes. The round or half-round files work around the curves of a cheekpiece or in the grip area with its compound curves. Although sometimes impossible, try to keep the rasps and files going with the direction of the grain in the wood. Excessive cross grain cutting of the wood fibers results in the need for extra elbow grease when the time comes for sanding. The compression and cutting trauma imparted to the wood fibers from rasping can go deeper than what is visible, so whenever possible try to go with the grain.

## File Handles

Regardless of what kind of work I'm doing, I always put a file handle on any file that has a tang.

File handles are available in wood or plastic and cost $2 to $3 each. These file handles are available in several sizes and come with bore diameters cut specifically for various file tangs.

The trick to getting a file tang to seat to full depth in a wood handle is start the tang into the handle by rapping it on your bench. After the file tang has started into the handle hole, hold the handle in your left hand and with an 8-ounce ball-peen hammer in your right hand whack the end of the handle until the tang seats to full depth.

Never pound on the end of the file. They are so brittle that damage may occur.

I don't remember exactly how many file handles I've put on using this technique, but my guess is over 100, and it always works.

I employ these types in shaping new stocks for the most common Remington and Winchester bolt-action rifles. I have my own stock patterns made from the lowest grade of walnut I can get. I then reshape these patterns to match the particular needs of the customer. It's a simple matter to build up an area with an auto-body filler, such as Bondo, to get the pattern as close to the customer's needs as possible and then

## Working Flat

One of the difficulties involved with filing is keeping the file flat and not rounding off edges. Whenever possible use a vise with square, flat, smooth faced jaws. I use one of the cheaply made drill press vises that has had the top of the vise jaws' surface ground so they are now true to one another. The inside faces have also been surface ground so that they too are flat. When a part that needs to be dressed with a file is placed between these jaws the file moves across the jaws and keeps the outside edges of the part from rounding over. Flatness is extremely important when dealing with sear surfaces and other parts that need to mate squarely.

File teeth are pitched forward and only cut when pushed forward.

send the pattern and stock blank off for profiling.

### File Shapes and Choices

Square, round, and triangular files each have their place when dealing with metal parts fitting.

A $^3/_{16}$-inch parallel round smooth cut file is just the ticket when fitting a

**Above:** *The sight-base file has two safe sides; they guide the file when cutting a dovetail wider.*

new barrel link on a 1911 style pistol. The radius on the barrel lugs of these style pistols is another place that needs attention when fitting a new barrel so that the slide stop pin rides over it allowing proper barrel lockup.

If you need to cut a dovetail for a sight but do not have access to a milling machine, spending less than $20 for a quarter-inch square file and sight base file will get you through this task. The square quarter inch file is used to remove the bulk of the metal, keeping the bottom of the future dovetail flat, level and perpendicular to the bore.

The sight base file is triangular shaped and has two safe sides that are used to undercut each end of the dovetail until the sight fits snugly in place. As the safe sides do not have teeth they are employed as guides to ride in the bottom of the dovetail while the side with teeth cuts. There are plenty of gun craftsmen who still use this method of installing sight dovetails and do a reputable job of it.

Needle files are hard to beat when the need for getting into tight places arises. These files are small enough so their size does not obliterate your ability to see what you are doing. Putting a slight chamfer on an extractor or the radiusing of the underside of a 1911 style extractor for case head clearance is where these files shine.

Of most use are the smaller 4 to 5 inch overall length files with 2 to $2^1/_2$ inches of cutting surface. The Swiss pattern files offer more grades of cut in the file teeth. For me, the #1 medium coarse, #2 medium, #3 medium fine, and the #4 fine serve particular well.

When dealing with the harder heat-treated steels sometimes found in gun parts, the fine-cut diamond needle files have enough stamina to remove burrs and sharp edges where a normal file wouldn't cut it.

## Care and Storage

Files should be kept separate from one another to prevent the teeth from clunking together. Haphazardly storing files in a cluster does nothing to preserve sharpness of their teeth. Files should also be dedicated to either metal or wood.

## Tip

If you need to remove an excessive amount of material, don't start with a file. Instead, scribe a line at the necessary depth and hacksaw the material above this scribed line. There isn't much sense wearing your arms out filing when there are quicker ways to remove the material.

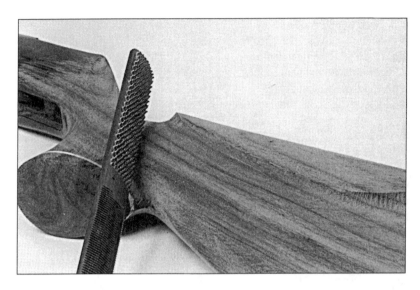

*Above: The horseshoe rasp has a curved side and a flat side. It comes in handy when roughing out gunstock shapes.*

## File Sizes and Thicknesses

Just as there are many different styles of files, there are different schools of thought on what sizes of files should be used. Control of the

*Above: The rat-tail file is quite handy for getting into small curved areas like those behind a grip cap.*

*Above: Pushing a file over a flat-topped vise will keep the edges of the part from rounding over.*

file becomes a factor, and for that reason my preference is for files with lengths of 4, 6, and 8 inches.

For me, it's much easier to feel what the file is doing when I'm using a size I can control. There are those who do quite well using the 10-, 12-, and 14-inch files.

For most of the part fitting I encounter I find myself reaching most of-

## Power Files

Using rotary files and burr bits in a motor-driven hand tool can add speed to your filing, especially on softer materials such as wood, but they also have application on metal.

A round, coarse burr bit, for instance, removes wood from a gunstock quickly in preparation for a glass bedding job.

Also, the cylinder and tapered carbide burr bits are handy for shaving metal, especially in hard-to-get-at areas. This works well when installing and blending flared magazine-well extensions on 1911s.

Additionally, small carbide ball burr bits are handy to use when a screw slot is butchered up, and you need to get the screw out for replacement. The little ball will cut a good enough slot so that the battered screw can be turned out.

ten for the pillar files in my rack. This type of file has a thicker body and therefore has less tendency to flex than some of the thinner files. The thicker, smaller files are also an asset when you need to keep the cut flat. Because most pillar files have safe sides, you don't have to worry when getting up against 90-degree shoulders that don't need undercutting.

When involving yourself with striking or draw filing barrels for tool mark removal or eliminating the pits caused by rust, a bigger file should get the call, mainly because you can get both hands on the file. This type of filing usually calls for much longer stokes with the determined effort to keep the work piece flat. Chalk the file to keep the file teeth from pinning or clogging up with the metal being removed and use a file card or brush to keep the file clean so it doesn't score the work.

When dealing with the roughing of stock shapes, I move up to the larger files. The 10-, 12-, and 14-inch rasps and files afford more width and length to hang onto when shaping a forearm or rounding the toe and heel on the butt. ★

# 3.

# Tools and Accessories
# For Stock Checkering

*Here are the items you'll want to make or
assemble before you take that first
pass with the gouge.*

*by Dennis A. Wood*

Checkering patterns are like snowflakes and deer antlers; no two are exactly alike. The reason checkering patterns are rarely the same is because gunstock forearms and grip areas are always somewhat different, especially with hand-shaped and hand-sanded stocks. It's extremely important that each pattern be tailored to the particular stock receiving the checkering adornment.

Even before you've applied the finish to the stock and allowed it to harden up properly, the checkering pattern can be conceived with the help of a few items. Unless you have very long arms, the center of the forearm checkering pattern will usually fall about $3^1/4$ to $3^1/2$ inches from the inletting in the stock, where the front edge of the receiver and barrel meet. This will give a forearm checkering pattern with a length of about $6^1/2$ inches to 7 inches. For normal use, this should accommodate most shooters off-hand.

I find a cloth or rubber-coated dressmaker's measuring tape to be helpful when conceiving ideas for the development of a checkering pattern on a forearm. This type of tape measure will wrap around the forearm and conform to the curves in the grip area—without danger of marring the surface finish. You'll only need the first 15 inches of this tape, as a whole tape length can get quite cumbersome. Some of these tapes come with a metal tip on the leading edge. I've removed the tip on the tape I use for fear that it might scratch the finish.

With the approximate target length of around 7 inches in mind, I wrap the tape around the forearm in the area where the receiver ring and the barrel meet. Note this dimension. Then, 7 inches forward, I once

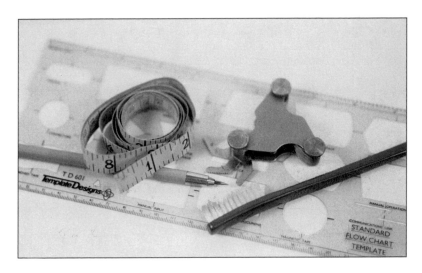

*Above:* A sharp scribe, a stiff-bristled brush, and a thread-pitch gauge are helpful.

again wrap the tape around the forearm and get this dimension. Measure from the top flat on one side of the forearm around to the top flat on the other side. Subtract ³/₈ inch from both of these dimensions. This will provide for a ³/₁₆-inch edge below both top sides of the forearm before the checkering pattern begins.

These dimensions can then be transferred to a piece of graph paper with 3.5:1 diamonds, with half the dimension going to the left of the centerline and the other half to the right. The front forearm dimension would be at the top of the graph paper and the rear dimension would go to the bottom of the paper, 7 inches below the top dimension.

I find it much easier to lay out or design the checkering pattern on the graph paper, rather than working on the stock itself. Changes or mistakes are much easier to correct with an eraser on the graph paper than they are to re-do on the stock. It's a simple matter to cut the pattern out with a scissors and wrap it around the stock to see what the design actually looks like on the forearm. You can then lay the pattern on the bench next to you for guidance when the time comes to actually begin cutting the checkering lines.

The grip area of a gunstock has compound curves which make the use of graph paper difficult. The graph paper can still be used for the design of a grip pattern, but keep in mind that it will not lay as flat to the surface as a pattern for the forearm will. The 3.5:1 diamond graph located inside the back cover can be photocopied as many times as you like. With the more sophisticated copy machines available for use at print shops and office-supply stores, you can reduce or enlarge the pattern slightly. Then sketch out your ideas until you get just what you want.

## Diamond Templates

The 3.5:1 ratio diamond has remained pretty much the same for the last 15 or 20 years. What this means is that each individual diamond created in the checkering process is 3.5 times longer than it is wide. Whenever possible, the 3.5 length should run parallel with the bore line. I've made up several size templates with this style of diamond to help with initial pattern layout, establishing the important master lines from which all the other lines will be spaced. These templates are made from 0.015-inch clear-plastic sheets. These $8^{1}/_{2}$- by 11-inch sheets can be purchased for less than a dollar from any hobby shop that sells supplies for radio-controlled model airplanes. These thin plastic templates can be wrapped around a forearm quite easily, yet still provide a stiff, straight edge for scribing.

To make a template, I start with the bottom $8^{1}/_{2}$-inch-wide edge. That way, you can be fairly sure you're starting with a straight line. You'll need a steel ruler, a sharp scribe, and a sharp blade in an X-acto knife. Start about $^{1}/_{4}$ inch from the left edge of the plastic sheet, and poke a dot with the scribe into the surface at the bottom edge. Measure $2^{1}/_{2}$ inches to the right, and poke another dot into the plastic sheet. Measure another $2^{1}/_{2}$ inches to the right, and again poke a dot into the plastic sheet. This will give the base of our template a width of 5 inches.

The next step is to poke a dot $8^{3}/_{4}$ inches up from the center dot at the base of the plastic sheet. It's very important to place this dot perpendicular to the bottom edge to prevent a lopsided template. Lay your straightedge ruler or a 90-degree steel square so that the scribe can be

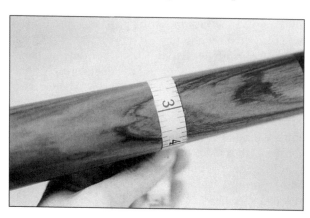

*Left:* When designing a forearm pattern, a dressmaker's tape can be wrapped around the stock to get the dimensions.

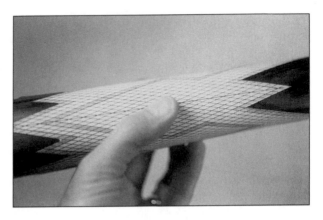

used to scratch a line from the bottom dot to the top dot. This centerline on the clear plastic sheet assists with alignment of the template on the forearm surface. Now lay the straightedge on the sheet, and connect the top dot to both the left and right dots on the bottom edge with a scribed line. Scratch these lines several times with added pressure on each pass to get them well defined. Then, with the straightedge as a cutting guide, use the X-acto knife to cut the template from the sheet. It is best to cut at least $1/4$ inch past the top dot on both sides to get a clean top point. If the scribed lines are deep enough, the knife blade will follow; the straightedge simply insures against any errant travel of the blade.

You should be able to get several different size diamond templates from a single sheet of plastic. I have made some that are smaller at the base in one-inch increments. These not only assist with the initial layout, but they act as gauges to ensure that spacing is going well when the actual checkering takes place. Beside the 3.5:1 diamond shape, other templates can be made for radii in the grip area, a small radiused point along the bottom of the grip area (just above the grip cap), and for the popular fleur-de-lis that is often seen in fill-in style patterns. ›

Some folks have good luck with decal templates. Once cut out, these can be placed on the stock in the area to receive the checkering. I once tried a decal for a simple pattern on a Ruger 10/22 stock. The forearm decal worked okay once I got it centered on the forearm, but the curves in the grip area gave me fits. Decals don't conform well in the grip area, and they often become wrinkled or torn in the positioning process. Another problem I've have with the decals is that water is required to remove the decal from the paper backing, and if you have a dry spot on the stock surface, the water will cause the area to swell slightly. I just don't bother with them any longer.

## Scribes, Blades, And Straightedges

Just about any good scribe will help with the basic layout of a checkering pattern on a gunstock, but those with a long tapering point seem to work best for me. A scribe point with an approximate angle of 10 degrees from the side will get the scribe tip up against your straightedge, and the actual point can never be too sharp. The scribe is used to lay out the all important master lines and provides the initial groove that your single-line cutter must follow.

An X-acto knife or one of the foreign copies of this handy little razor blade cutter is beneficial when cutting radii for a fleur-de-lis or around a plastic template such as those for a point at the bottom of a grip above the grip cap.

A straightedge is another of those important items that will assist in the layout of your checkering patterns. I've tried several different types of straightedges made of plastic and thin steel, and have found that, whatever the material, the length should be at least 10 inches and the material no thicker than around 0.035 inch. A flexible straightedge can be twisted and turned into a corkscrew configuration, yet the edge remains straight. One of the straightedges I use is made of clear green plastic with drafting symbols die cut into it. These can be purchased in most any office-supply store. If you have a broken steel measuring tape, a 10-inch section of the tape can be used for a straightedge. It's best to back the concave surface with tape so that the surface finish on the gunstock will not be scratched. I've also tried the thick plastic banding used to secure large items transported on wood pallets. The things to keep in mind when choosing a straight edge are that the edge must be truly straight, and the material must be flexible enough to wrap around a forearm without buckling up and causing a kink in the edge.

A flexible plastic French curve is a common tool used by draftsmen

*Left:* A curved-point template can be used for the border at the bottom of the grip and the radius at the rear of the grip pattern.

who aren't yet caught up in the age of CAD (computer-assisted drafting). The French curve can be helpful when scribing curved borders in the grip area, or when blending the curves on fill-in patterns on the forearm.

## Convenient Helpmates

Sometimes, to complete a repair or restoration, a new forearm must be made and checkered with the same style of pattern found on the stock, or vice versa. This is usually no big deal, but you will need to determine what the spacing of the checkering is so that it can be reproduced on the new wood. I find that a thread-pitch gauge works just fine to determine checkering spacing. The thread-pitch gauge has leaves with 60-degree teeth that will measure any previous checkering cut from 16 to 32 lines per inch. When spacing new checkering, the thread-pitch gauge will also aid with the inspection of lines and help keep the diamond widths even.

Some gunsmiths find it helpful to place temporary borders around a checkering pattern to help guide them with layout. Methods used to define these temporary borders include the use of tape or grease pencil. Most grease pencils produce a line that's really too thick for my purposes, but the white or yellow "mark on anything" pencils that Brownells sells can produce a temporary border guide that is crisp and easily removed when no longer needed. These pencils can be sharpened in an ordinary pencil sharpener.

Use care in selecting a tape for defining a temporary checkering border. Some tapes are strong enough to lift the finish from the stock surface when removed. While I don't use it often, I've found that most cellophane-type tapes will work quite well, and won't lift the surface finish.

And finally, one of the handiest gadgets for checkering can be found in your medicine cabinet—an old toothbrush. Checkering produces quite a bit of dust during the cutting process, and a toothbrush will keep the furrows between the diamonds clean as you progress. Use an old toothbrush if you have one, or, if you don't, be sure to use your wife's. If you go out and buy one just for this purpose, I think you'll find that the stiffer the bristles, the better it will work.  ★

*Right: A fleur-de-lis template helps with scribing the outline of the flower.*

# 4.

# Make Your Own Sight-Drilling Fixture

*Why buy a commercial sight-drilling fixture when you can fashion one with scraps for about an eighth of the cost?*

*By Dennis Wood*

Try as they might, it seems like firearms manufacturers just can't please all of the people all of the time.

Not all that long ago, sporting rifles were brought to the shop to have their open sights removed. The job usually involved removing some screws that held the sights on, then filling the tapped holes left behind in the barrel with a few plug screws. In extreme cases, the sights had to be heated up enough to soften the solder before they would come off. The bare metal beneath the sights usually needed a touch-up blueing. The idea, of course, was to use just the rifle with a scope sight and forego the open sights.

I suppose the rifle manufacturers figured that if no open sights were wanted, none would be provided. A few models offer a choice of sighting systems, giving you open sights or a set of rings and bases. Few manufacturers give you both. But some shooters want the option of both sights and scope, which usually means the barrel needs to be drilled and tapped for the open-sight option, if barrel thickness allows. This isn't a difficult job but, as is so often the case, the sight-drilling job (always an emergency!) would come in just when I had my mill tied up with another task.

What I needed was a fixture to drill the mounting holes for sights quickly and accurately, something that would let me accommodate the occasional owner always in a hurry. The fixture would have to be set up quickly, used with a drill press, and be capable of drilling precisely located mounting holes for sights or scope bases.

Commercial fixtures, and their accessories, are sold just for this pur-

**Above:** *With a barreled action in place, holes for scope bases or sights can be drilled accurately.*

pose. I've also priced them. With drill bushings and the extensions needed to do longer barrels, the things can run close to $400.

You don't have to spend that kind of money. I made up my own fixture, spending less than an eighth of what a commercial rig costs. The only items I had to shell out hard cash for were the hardened steel drill bushings, three cold-rolled steel side rails and, obviously, all the bolts. All the other materials were end cuts from a local machine shop. I've said it before, you need to get acquainted with the shop foremen or owners. You'd be amazed at the useful stuff some of these shops discard. You might have to pay scrap steel prices for some of it, but it's still usually cheap.

More than likely, they'll ask what you are doing. Your answer could mean a continued supply of end cut stock.

Three rails, all made of cold-rolled steel, are involved on this sight drilling fixture. They are each $5/16$ inch thick by $1^1/2$ inches high by 34 inches long and have 15 letter "V" size holes drilled through them. When I drilled the letter V holes, I laid out just one rail for the hole positions and center punched the spacing for the holes. I then placed the other two rails beneath the top one so the spacing would be the same for all three.

Beginning 2 inches from the left end of each rail is a series of nine holes, 1 inch apart. Sixteen inches from the left end is a series of three holes, 1 inch apart. Another series of three holes, also an inch apart, is

25 inches from the left end. These holes are for spacing adjustments to the base blocks. All the letter" V" holes have been chamfered with an 82-degree countersink tool so that the $^3/_8$-16 Allen head machine screws will fit flush with the side rails.

The three base blocks are made of magnesium, which happened to be the end cuts locally available at the time. Magnesium machines beautifully and if it were the only material your cutting tools ever saw, they would last indefinitely. There are some drawbacks to machining magnesium. The fine chips and shavings produced are highly flammable and can be easily ignited by a spark, which is why magnesium should be your last choice. Aluminum is better.

The base blocks give the whole fixture stability. All three blocks measure 5 inches deep from front rail to back rail, 2 inches thick by $3^1/_2$ inches high. There is a 1 inch through hole in each of the base blocks. The hole in each block is on the top centerline, 1 inch from either side and $1^1/_4$ inch from the back of the block. These holes accept the 1- inch diameter round shanks for the barrel holding v-blocks. On the face of each of these blocks, on a centerline to the 1-inch through hole, a $^3/_8$-16 hole has been tapped through into the 1-inch hole. This is for height adjusting and holding screws that help level a barreled action once it is clamped into place.

At the front of each block, there is a slot milled to half depth for a steel rectangular section of key stock. The key stock is a 0.312 inch square that rests on top of the front rail and acts as a stop. All these keys are machine screwed into the magnesium blocks. At the rear of each block, a slot is milled to half depth to accept a steel key measuring 0.500 inch high by 0.375 inch thick. These slot centerlines are milled $1^7/_8$ inch from the top of the blocks. Each of the keys is attached with one #10-32 machine screw. These keys act as stops between the two back rails, and slide fore and aft when adjusting the fixture for length.

The leveling and clamp holding screws are each $^3/_8$-16 with a 1-inch washer silversoldered onto its head. Three small holes are drilled through each washer 120 degrees apart so small wood screws can be used to attach a larger turning knob. These large knobs give a better grip when tightening the screws in place. The knobs, turned out of American Black Walnut scrap pieces left over from a gun stock blank, have a diameter of 2 inches and a thickness of 1 inch.

Two v-block rests also act as clamps to hold a barreled action during the drilling and tapping operations. The clamps are also made out of magnesium and are 1-inch thick. On the 1 inch centerline and $1^1/_4$ inches from the rear of the v-block, a 0.500 inch hole is drilled to a depth of 1 inch. There is a 1 inch shaft made of cold-rolled steel for each of the v-blocks, along with one for the flat platform rest at the other end of this fixture. All three of these round shafts have an overall length of 4 inches.

One end of each shaft was turned down to a diameter of 0.501 inch, for a length of ¹/₂ inch so the end would press fit into the 0.500 inch hole in the v-block and platform base for it. On all three of these one inch shafts, a 3-degree flat was milled from the bottom end of the shaft up toward the top. The ³/₈-16 holding and height adjusting screws do a better job with this slight angle than they do with just a straight flat. The slot at the bottom of each "v" serves the dual purpose of relieving the bottom of the v-block of any radius as well as creating some clearance for milling the sides of the v- block.

Two smaller v-blocks that fit inside the main actors are adaptors for those ultra-light sporter rifles with barrel diameters roughly equal to vermicelli pasta. At the top of each v-block, there is a clamp that maintains downward pressure to hold the barrel in place. Both clamps are slip fit mounted to a ⁵/₁₆-18 tpi threaded stud. At the back of each top clamp, a ⁵/₁₆-18 tpi bolt is inverted so that the head of the bolt butts up against the base of the clamp. This bolt gives stability to the clamp and adjusts it for height. The lock down nut for the clamp is made out of ³/₄-inch cold-rolled steel stock that had a through hole threaded in the center for the ⁵/₁₆-18 threaded stud. The threaded studs are cut from ⁵/₁₆-18 threaded stock to an overall length of 3 inches, with 0.75 inch going into the clamp base and permanently fixed in place with thread sealant. Two 0.3125-inch steel handles are brazed onto the lock down nut to aid quick removal and tightening. A washer is in between the nut and clamp.

The third block holds the leveling platform for the rear of the rifle action and acts as a support. This block measures 2³/₄ inches long, 1³/₄ inches wide, and 0.750 inch thick. It is also attached to a 1-inch shaft made in the same manner as the two for each v-block. This platform acts as a leveling device, making sure that the drilled holes go into the barrel or receiver perpendicular to the bore line. Most actions have some sort of flat on the bottom like a magazine cutout or, in the case of the Mauser 98 and Winchester Model 70, the bottom of the receiver itself. I met an owner who wanted his 22-inch barreled Remington 742 rifle cut to resemble the 18¹/₂-inch carbine model. This meant that the front sight would need to be reattached to the barrel. Removing the trigger group and magazine after complete disassembly produced the flat area that was needed to drill the holes for the front sight.

A through hole in the center top of this platform, 0.500-inch for the 1-inch shaft, is the same as those in the v-blocks. The end of the 1-inch shaft for the platform has a ¹/₄-20 hole tapped into it for the attachment of a flat piece of stock that goes on top of an action to anchor it and minimize any side-to-side movement.

An overarm with a bushing plate is made up next. The bushing plate, also made of magnesium end cuts, is $3^1/_2$ inches long, $3^1/_4$ inches wide, and $^3/_4$ inch thick. There are three bushing liners press fitted in place on the exact centerline of the v-blocks. The liners are steel sleeves that receive interchangeable drill bushings for the #45, #28 and #31 drill bits used for most sight and scope base threaded attachment holes. Drill bushings guide the drill to prevent any walking or wobbling of the drill bit. Three liners are in place on this bushing plate, spaced 0.504 inch and then 0.860 inch apart, the most common spacings encountered when installing scope bases.

On the bottom of this bushing plate at the back edge, a 0.750 inch slot was milled 0.250-inch deep to accept the upright support plate that attaches to the rear rails. Two $^1/_4$-20 hex head machine bolts go down through this top bushing plate and secure it to the top end of the support plate. The support plate measures 7 inches high by $3^1/_2$ inches wide by 0.750-inch thick and is also made of magnesium.

On a centerline $1^1/_2$ inches from the bottom of the support plate, a slot was milled 0.500 inch wide to accept a square piece of steel key stock that rides between the two rear rails of the fixture base. Two

**Above:** *The overarm bushing plate can be adjusted forward and backward for hole spacing.*

through holes were drilled in this key support plate 2³/₈ inches from one another to accept ⁵/₁₆-18 bolts, which attach to two t-nuts that tighten the support arm to the two rear rails.

Once a barreled action is clamped and leveled in the v-blocks, this over arm bushing plate can be moved along the rear of the fixture until the drill bushings are over the top of the action or barrel where the holes are to be placed. By using drill bushings to guide a spinning drill, you are less likely to get drill "walk", especially when trying to drill into a radius like you find when dealing with the top of a barrel or receiver ring.

When drilling sight base holes in a barrel and usually in the receiver ring, we often need to tap into a blind hole drilled to a specific depth so as not to break through into the bore or chamber area. When drilling blind holes that need tapping, I use a 135-degree split point drill bit tip. A 165-degree tip would be better, but drills are not readily available with this flat an angle so it would have to be custom ground. The most common drill bit cutting angle is 118 degrees, but the 135 drill bit angle will cut better in harder steels.

The bottom taps used to cut threads into blind holes have a short lead or cutting edge ground to a 30-35 degree angle on the first 1¹/₂ to 2 teeth. Using the flatter cutting 135-degree drill bit, then a bottom tap, will give one or two more complete threads, which means more holding ability for the screw going through the sight base and into the cut threads. The reason most sight screws are so finely threaded is that they will hold in thinner material, so the more threads per inch the better. If the threads are to go completely through, as on the receiver bridge of a bolt action rifle, then the normal 118-degree drill will work just fine along with a plug style tap with the seven degree cutting lead.

The tapping operation on any hole requires attention to get the tap started in straight. If the tap starts crooked, it may break and the head of the screw will not hold down the sight base evenly. It also looks just plain amateurish.

Most t-handle tap wrenches have a 60-degree center cut into the end of the wrench body by the sliding t-handle. A small 60-degree male center chucked in your drill press will go into the female center in the t-handle wrench. Use this option to get the tap started in straight, at least until three or four full threads have been cut. A good grade of cutting oil on the tap delays its dulling and cuts cleaner threads.

When making this fixture, I tried to envision all the possibilities involved with drilling and tapping various makes and models of rifles and shotguns for sights and scope bases. I have yet to encounter any that wouldn't work with this rig. ★

# 5.

# Build an OD Grinder
# For Less Than $150

*If you've ever needed an OD grinder, but balked
at paying $2,000 to $3,000 for one, try this easily
constructed do-it-yourself model.*

*by Chip Todd*

There are times when every gunsmith finds the need to reduce the diameter of something round. That's no problem if the gunsmith has, or can afford to buy, an OD (outside diameter) grinder. Unfortunately, an OD grinder is expensive, and is unlikely to be found except in a completely equipped machine shop.

I have frequently needed to reduce the diameters of hardened-steel pins, end-mill cutters, and other items that couldn't be done on my lathe. That's why I started thinking about the need for an affordable OD grinder for use on carbon and stainless steels. (Brass and aluminum will load up a stone's surface quickly; instead, use a disk grinder for aluminum or brass.)

An OD grinder is a grinder which is set up with some type of feed/rotator mechanism allowing the outside diameter of a round object to be reduced by grinding concentric with the main axis of the part. The part is held in a collet, and is rotated while in contact with a grinding wheel. All good OD grinders have some method of moving the workpiece back and forth along its axis while it is rotating so that the outside diameter remains coaxial with the other diameters along the workpiece. Most machine shops use a surface grinder to do all of the work with the exception of rotating the workpiece. Like our economy version detailed here, the rotating is done with some sort of rotary indexer or other spinning mechanism.

## Acquiring the Components

To make our OD grinder, we need a baseplate, a bench grinder, an x-y positioning table, a rotary indexer, and collets. These are usually

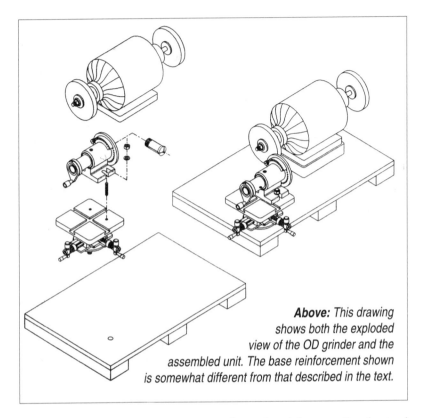

**Above:** *This drawing shows both the exploded view of the OD grinder and the assembled unit. The base reinforcement shown is somewhat different from that described in the text.*

available from local tool marts or can be ordered from mail-order tool houses. Total cost should be under $150, which is a tiny fraction of the cost of a commercially built model.

To start with the largest part, the bench grinder is the same type you see in Sears, designed to fit onto a workbench, usually with two screws. The minimum size that I would suggest is a 6-inch grinder, although you could substitute patience for grinder size, if preferred. I use a 6-inch grinder with a ³/₄-inch-wide stone, although a ¹/₂-inch stone would suffice. I prefer the dark-gray stone, but the white grinder stones work well, too. A half-horse motor is sufficient, and I chose one which had an integral switch, but this isn't necessary. I've seen decent grinders in tool marts for around $35, and some that appear adequate for as low as $25.

The next part is the positioning table, which has two slideways. The slideways are perpendicular to each other in a horizontal arrangement. These are also called a "cross slide" or "milling and drilling" table, and can be found anywhere from $35 to $1,500. It is necessary to get one which has two perpendicular slides, which also makes it a "compound table." The top slide is to be mounted parallel, but not coaxial with the axis of the grinder, and the lower slide is the transverse one, for ease of use. Each slide is controlled by a crank which has as little play as possible. Better slideways have "gibs," which are tapered strips of metal that can be advanced into the two dovetailed ways to remove play from between them. Cheaper ones, like the one I use, have set screws to remove the play. The set screws should be brass, or they will screw up the side surface of the slide.

Positioning tables differ in mounting. Some have a central post, while others have flanges with holes or slots for mounting screws. The one I use has a $3/4$-inch post on the bottom—not that it's any better than the others. A spin (rotary) indexer is a colleted fixture which holds a 5C collet parallel to its base, and spins it about its axis. A flange behind the collet has holes arranged in a vernier fashion to allow a pin to index the workpiece in 1-degree increments.

The accuracy of these indexers is usually within $1/2$ degree. The collet is held in and tightened by a threaded tube, which is turned and tightened by a crank on the rear opposite the collet. The collet is kept from spinning during the tightening process by placing the indexing pin into any hole, while the crank is turned to clamp down on the workpiece. A spin indexer, also called an "indexing spin jig," should cost between $35 and $100.

A collet is a cylindrical clamp for the workpiece which has a precise hole in its axis with three or four slits radiating from the central hole. The 5C collets are tapered behind the front and threaded externally at the rear for a drawbar. The drawbar draws the collet into a tapered hole in the indexer, thereby tightening down the opening onto the workpiece. These 5C collets are usually used on lathes, and are different from the internally threaded R8 collets typically used on milling machines. Collets should cost anywhere from $6 to $25, depending on where you look. The standard-type grinding wheels that come with most bench grinders will suffice for this grinder, and I wouldn't spend any extra money for another stone before you use the OD grinder and see what type finish you can get. Wheels only cost about $5 from the discount tool houses.

The baseplate can be anything from steel or aluminum plate to $3/4$-inch plywood. You will find that a $3/8$-inch-thick metal plate will make a more stable platform, but I have used an OD grinder with a $3/4$-inch plywood base for over 15 years without any trouble grinding to the accuracy necessary. If plywood is used, it is a good idea to reinforce it with some substantial framework beneath it. I believe in gluing all wood joints, whether they need it or not. I only leave a wood joint unglued if

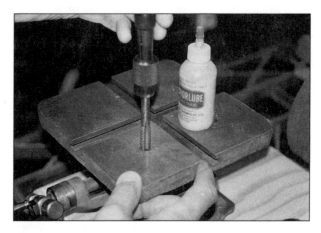

*Right: Tap ⁷/₁₆-14 threads in two places on the x-y positioning table for the studs or screws holding the rotary indexer. Note the lateral slide-crank handle in the left foreground.*

the pieces are going to be disassembled. And I never use wood screws. I prefer machine screws or bolts against threaded metal inserts.

## Assembling the OD Grinder

I couldn't wait until I ran across a piece of suitable metal for the baseplate, so I decided to make the base from ³/₄-inch plywood. I started out by laying the components (spin-indexer, grinder, x-y table, and collets) out in the configuration that would do the work. I then measured the outside dimensions that would confine the group and cut a piece of ³/₄-inch fir plywood to that size (12 x 20 inches). I then reinforced the bottom with a framework of 2x4 pieces. The accompanying drawing shows a simpler base made of three pieces of 2x4 and a piece of higher-quality for the base.

Having bought and used both an x-y table and a spin-indexer on my mill and 5C collets on my lathe, I realized that I had the ingredients for an OD grinder already in my shop. I just needed to assemble them in a way that would facilitate precision grinding of diameters. I also had an extra bench grinder, so all I would need would be to make a baseplate and a small riser for the grinder.

Being right-handed, I arranged the components so that they were in a natural location for the crank-turning that I knew I would need to do. This meant that the x-y table needed to be on the left with the cranks to the left and the front, while the grinder would be toward the rear and right. Since the grinder I was to be using had a centerline about 5 inches from its base, and the combination of the x-y table with the spin indexer on top would place the centerline of the workpiece at about 7 inches, I knew I would have to space the grinder up about 2 inches for it to work properly. Placing the workpiece below the centerline of the grindstone would make any incremental marks on the lateral crank's hub read wrong. While I rarely use these marks, as they are often no more than rough approximations on cheap equipment, I still have a tendency to follow such little pieces of good machine-shop practice.

My method of mounting the x-y table required that I bore a $^3/_4$-inch hole for the threaded stud that stuck downward to mount the device to the base. Because the crank handles would need some height over the worktable so that I wouldn't scrape my knuckles on the bench, I decided to space up the baseplate plywood with some pieces of 2x4.

My next step was to determine where on the x-y table the spin-indexer should be mounted. I knew that it should be on the forward edge of the top surface so that it would be near the side where the grinder would be, so I picked the forward and proximal edge to the proposed grinder location. After marking where the mounting bolt holes should be, I mounted the x-y table onto my drill press and, using the x-y table's own alignment capabilities, I drilled the .368-inch-diameter (Q-size drill) pilot holes for the $^7/_{16}$-14 threads.

I used the tap guides that are made for drill presses and tapped each hole before I moved the x-y table from the drilling locations. After tapping the holes in the table's top, I slightly counterbored the tops of the threaded holes and used a flat file to file away any burrs which were proud of (above) the top surface.

After mounting the x-y table onto the baseplate with the large washer and nut, I bolted the spin-indexer onto it with some $^7/_{16}$ NC studs and nuts. Three-eighths-16 threaded holes and screws should work just as well, but the spin indexer I used had been slotted for larger screws. It shouldn't matter much whether you use studs and hex nuts, hex-head or hex-socket cap screws; just use something that can be tightened up

**Left:** *Dress the surface of the grinding wheel with a stone-dressing block or, as shown here, with a homemade dressing-point holder in a $^1/_2$-inch 5C collet.*

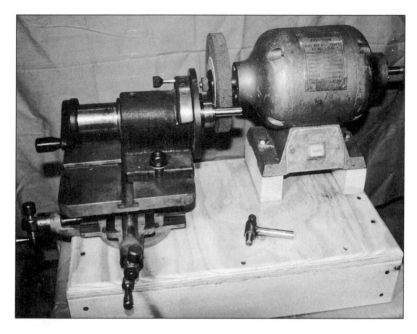

**Above:** *The finished OD grinder is shown here with a ¹/₂-inch hardened pin in the collet ready to be ground. Note the dressing point and holder in the foreground. The index-locking pin can be seen protruding to the left on the top of the spin indexer.*

very tightly. As is always good practice, I used some thick flat washers between the base flange of the spin-indexer and the nuts so that the nuts wouldn't bite into the sides of the mounting slots.

It is essential to have the axis of the spin indexer parallel to the longitudinal axis of the cross slide table. Otherwise, the grinding will not be cylindrical, but rather will be tapered. This can be done either on the grinding machine or on a workbench. There are any number of good ways to ensure that they're parallel; the best way is to actually grind something on the finished machine and measure it along its length while adjusting the indexer's position, until the workpiece is consistent in diameter for the length you need in accuracy. It is more important that the spin indexer be parallel to the slide than it is for the slide to be perpendicular to the grinder's axis. The dressing stone will make a grinding wheel surface which is absolutely parallel to the slide's ways.

The only important thing about mounting the bench grinder to the baseplate is that the axis of the grinder be approximately the same height as the workpiece. It was necessary to space mine up about 2 inches to achieve this, so I cut some fir blocks. I drilled one hole in each block to accept $^5/_{16}$ NC threaded brass inserts so that the vibrations from the grinding wouldn't wallow out the screw holes. After inserting the threaded inserts, I drilled for two long wood screws in each base piece to hold them down until the glue dried. (Actually, there was no reason to remove the screws, so I left them in.)

The CAD drawing shows the grinder without any safety guards. If you can, however, I would suggest that you leave the guards on and remove the tool rests and any other protuberances that would get in the way of the workpiece. My removal of the guards on the CAD drawing is done for viewing simplification, and is not an endorsement of safety-guard removal.

In deciding where the grinder was going to be located, I mounted the x-y table and indexer, and put a collet and workpiece in it. I then adjusted the longitudinal slide to the middle of its travel, and the transverse slide near its rearward extreme. I had chosen a fairly small-diameter workpiece to use for this, as it was easier to use in locating the cross-travel location. With the slide almost all the way to the right in the x direction, (side-to-side from the operator's view), and the lower slide within $^1/_2$ inch of its rearward travel, I placed the motor-mounting blocks, with the motor mounted on them, to a position which put it parallel to the rear edge of the baseplate and the grinding wheel's surface against the workpiece.

I then marked the locations of the mounting blocks, took them off of the motor, and glued and screwed them into place.

## Dressing the Wheel

For dressing the grinding wheel, you can use either a primitive or a complex device, depending on your facilities. A simple holding fixture to secure a stone-dressing block will suffice, or you can make a shaft to hold a single-point diamond dressing tool in the collet. Either way, the idea is for the dressing point to dress the grinding stone's surface parallel to the travel of the longitudinal slide. I welded a sleeve perpendicular to a $^1/_2$-inch rod, tapped a hole in the sleeve for a set screw, and used a single-point dressing tool in this primitive holder.

Once all the parts are in place, it's time to dress the stone's edge and align the cross slide travel. With the grinder running, lock the indexer so that it won't rotate, and move the longitudinal slide so that the dresser is away from the grinding wheel. The lateral feed slide should also be moved until the dresser is just shy of allowing the dresser to touch the stone.

With the grinder on, advance the dressing point across the surface of the grinding wheel, making sure you crank the slide evenly. Use the lateral feed (front-to-back) slightly to take a little bit more from the surface of the grinding wheel. Do this until the surface is flat and even across the entire surface of the stone. This will ensure that the stone is perfectly round and parallel to the longitudinal slide of the x-y table.

## Operating the OD Grinder

To load the workpiece into the OD grinder, insert a collet of the proper size for the round workpiece you want to grind into the spin indexer, making sure that any keyway in the collet catches a peg (if it exists) in the indexer. Not all indexers have this feature. Pushing the collet into the indexer with one hand, crank the spindle handle at the rear with the other hand to engage the threads of the collet with the spindle. Now insert the workpiece before the collet starts getting squeezed down by the spindle. The spin indexer's small locking pin needs to be engaged with any of the holes in the base's flange and a hole in the rotating disk, ensuring that the collet is drawn up into the spindle's taper, thereby tightening the workpiece into the collet.

When using the OD grinder, the only thing to remember is to keep the indexer spinning whenever the workpiece is in contact with the grinding wheel. To start in reducing the outside diameter of the workpiece, the positioning table is moved away from the stone in both directions until the workpiece is slightly away from the stone's surface. I would move the longitudinal slide so that the area of the workpiece that needs grinding is in front of the stone, and the front-to-rear clearance is about $1/16$ inch. Then, while rotating the workpiece with the spin indexer, the lateral slide is moved so that the workpiece is barely in contact with the turning stone. A very slight spray of sparks should be thrown off of the stone, accompanied by a hissing sound. Continue with this spinning and advancing the workpiece until the spray of sparks is continuous, meaning that the stone has ground the workpiece round and concentric with the rest of the workpiece. This grinding isn't like sharpening a chisel on a grindstone. It needs to be done with a very light grinding and the spin indexer should never be stopped while the stone is in contact with the workpiece. The advancing of the lateral (feed) slide should be so slight that the work never gets hot, since it can conduct grinding heat away through the collet into the spin indexer.

The workpiece should be measured quite often, using dial calipers or a micrometer. The final several thousandths needs to be removed by using such a light cut that sparks are almost nonexistent. It will only take a few minutes to develop a good feel for this type of grinding, so practice on some spare round stock. ★

# 6.

# Build a Better, Cheaper Portable Shooting Bench

*Here's a shooting surface that's superior to any other carryable unit you can buy, and it is much less expensive.*

*by Walt Netzel*

Store-bought portable shooting benches are expensive, and most are not as good as even a marginal permanent wood stand. Some have small rectangular platforms, with no elbow support. Some are unstable due to small footprints and flexible platforms. Many are heavy, time-consuming to assemble, and require two hands to carry to the range.

The portable shooting bench detailed here weighs only 23 pounds. It will stand on edge when clamped in the carrying mode, and will fit into a small luggage compartment. (The longest piece is only 44 inches long.) It takes less than four minutes to assemble on the range. It's almost as good as a concrete bench. The platform won't flex; it's 2 ¹/₂ inches thick. The footprint is a 6-foot circle, stable on any surface—soft ground, plowed fields, or smooth concrete. You sit on a stool attached to one leg, with your weight distributed to all three legs. After removing the legs—they're held on with wing nuts—the portable shooting bench collapses to a package that easily fits into the trunk of a car. A handle allows you to carry it to the range with one hand. And a unique feature that you won't find on any other bench keeps your ammunition from rolling off the platform.

If you have a table saw, or have access to one, you can build this portable shooting bench in a few hours. All it takes is one-third of a sheet of ¹/₂-inch A-C plywood, two 2x4s, and some nuts and bolts. It should cost about $15. If you need to cut some corners, you can even use ³/₈-inch plywood. I used cedar 2x4s to keep the weight down and because they were free of knots. The legs should be cut from clear stock;

**Above:** *At a fraction of the cost and weight of the store-bought models, the do-it-yourself portable shooting bench can add consistency and convenience to your testing of new or repaired firearms.*

knots could weaken them. Except for the bolted leg joints, everything is glued together. I used yellow carpenters' glue. (White glue isn't very strong, and it's not water resistant.) The legs are bolted on with 10 $5/16$-inch carriage bolts. Wing nuts and washers are also required. It's a good idea to finish the bench with several coats of varnish; it might get rained on sometime.

Start by cutting the top and bottom of the bench platform from the plywood. Be careful to lay out the pattern so both "A" sides will be out. I used a saber saw (jig saw) to cut the rounded corners to a 2-inch radius. Remember to leave enough room on the inside corner to cut the 2-inch radius. The spacers between the plywood top and bottom are cut from 1 $1/2$ by 1$5/8$-inch stock—half of a 2x4. The photo shows the layout. The spacers need a good glue joint. Avoid large knots, they will bulge slightly and make a poor glue joint. Glue the long and perimeter spacers to the bottom first. Then glue the two short internal spacers; these should be centered 7$3/4$ inches from the front and back outside edges of the platform (so the leg bolts will go through them). If you don't have clamps large enough to reach to the internal spacers, use wood screws through clearance holes in the plywood to hold the joints until the glue sets. Before you glue the top to the spacers, run a plane over the spacers to make sure they make a flat surface. Let the perimeter spacers extend just slightly beyond the edge of the plywood. That way, it will be easier to clean up the glue joint with a saw or plane.

This bench is built to be used with a rifle rest. It holds the butt of the rifle about 6 inches above the platform. If you're going to support your rifle on sandbags, the platform needs to be higher. This design puts the platform 30 inches high. Most sandbag users will want the platform about 36 inches high, with the stool height still at 16 inches. To raise the platform, you can extend the two right legs $8^{3}/_{8}$ inches, but that won't work for the left leg. (The stool will be too high.) Instead, redesign the leg with more bend in it so the platform can be 6 inches higher without raising the stool.

Build the stool leg first; you will need it in place when you cut the rear right leg's plate, because the two plates are close together. The stool leg or left leg is cut from $1^{1}/_{2}$ by $2^{1}/_{2}$-inch stock, ripped from a 2x4. The shallow angle of the scarf can be cut with the aid of a scrap of plywood with parallel edges. Draw the line to be cut on the work and nail the plywood edge to the line with two small wire nails. Set your fence to just clear the plywood, and use the fence to guide the plywood and the work past the blade. When you have finished, pull the plywood off the work (see photo above). To make the scarf joint, use two wire nails at each end, driven only $^{1}/_{4}$ inch into the bottom piece before applying the glue. Pull the pieces apart and apply the glue, fit the nails back into the same holes they came from, and finish driving them in.

**Above:** *This inside view of the platform shows the spacer arrangement. Note that both long spacers run the entire length of the platform.*

**Figure 1, this page and opposite.**
**Left Leg Side View, Parts Details**

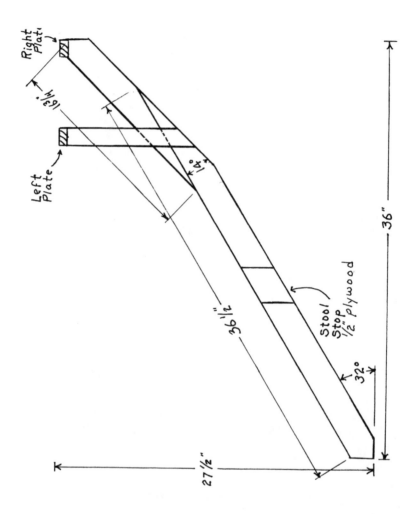

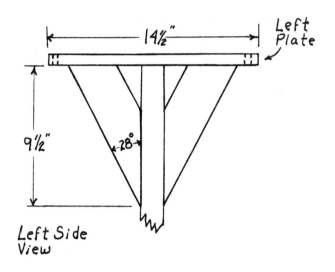

14½"

Left Plate

9½"

28°

Left Side View

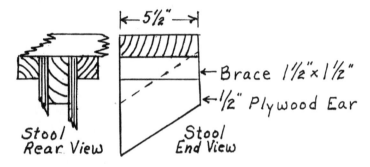

5½"

Brace 1½"x1½"

½" Plywood Ear

Stool Rear View

Stool End View

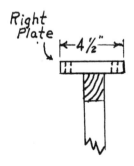

Right Plate

4½"

**Figure 2. Right Rear Leg and Plate Top and Side Views**

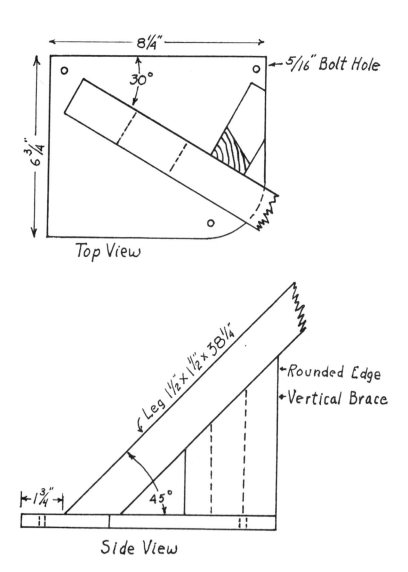

Top View

Side View

**Figure 2. Right Rear Leg and Plate Front View**

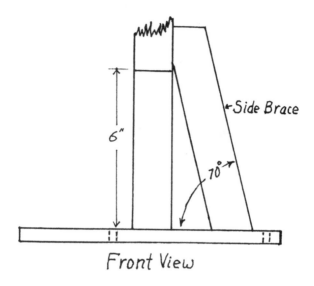

Front View

You can now apply the clamps and nothing will slip.

The stool leg is glued to two plates, and the plates are bolted to the platform. I used a $4^1/_2$ by $1^1/_2$ by $^3/_4$-inch piece of hardwood for the front plate. It's under a lot of tension, so cedar may fail here, but you can use cedar for the larger rear plate. It's a good idea to drill the bolt holes in these two plates before you start the glue joints. Clamp the smaller plate to the platform before you glue it to the leg, and then use it for a template to drill the $^5/_{16}$-inch bolt holes in the platform. It should be $8^1/_2$ inches from the back edge of the platform.

The end grain of all three legs is glued to a plate. To make a secure end-grain glue joint, smear a thin coat of glue on the end and let it dry. This will raise the wood fibers and leave a rough surface. Then sand the raised fibers off with fine sandpaper and proceed with a normal glue joint. If you don't seal the end grain with a preliminary coat of glue, too much of the subsequent coat of glue will soak into the wood, leaving a glue-starved joint. Use this procedure to glue the small hardwood plate to the top of the stool leg. Even a well-made glue joint in this position needs to be reinforced. You can use four wood screws. Drill countersunk clearance holes in the plate for them. If you use small diameter "sheet rock" screws, you won't have to drill body holes in

the cedar leg. In any case, use screws at least $2^1/_2$ inches long. Another choice is to use a stove bolt and a T-nut to reinforce this glue joint.

The rear plate is $14^1/_2$ by 1 $^1/_2$ by $^3/_4$ inches. This piece doesn't need to be hardwood. Start by cutting the diagonal bracing. Make the shallow angle cuts on the bracing first. Then square your miter and hold the shallow angle cut against the miter to make the second cut. This is the easy way to assure that the two cuts are at right angles. Glue the braces to the plate first, using a scrap of the leg material for a spacer between them. It's a good idea to reinforce this joint with screws, too.

Next bolt the small front plate to the platform. Be gentle with it; the glue joint won't support the weight of the leg at this stage. Slide the large rear plate with the braces into position and clamp this assembly to the platform. Make sure there is no torque on the front plate, and fasten the braces to the leg with two wood screws on each side (predrilled clearance holes will help). Mark the position of the braces on the sides of the leg with a pencil line to help reposition them. The leg with attached braces can then be removed from the platform. Remove the screws and glue the braces to the leg using the pencil lines and screw holes to reposition them. The screws are also used to apply pressure on the glue joint.

Both left-side legs are fastened to plates made of $^1/_2$-inch plywood. The plates measure $6^3/_4$ by $8^1/_4$ inches. Cut the front corners of both plates to match the 2-inch radius of the platform corners. The legs are cut from a 2x4, and are $1^1/_2$ inches square and $38^1/_4$ inches long, measured from bevel to bevel (actually about 40 inches overall). Cut both ends to a 45-degree bevel; the ends should be parallel. Trim enough off the tip of the bottom ends to leave a square bottom. The vertical brace is cut from a 2x4; it should be 6 inches long at the front edge. Glue the brace to the plate on a line that is 30 degrees from the inside edge of the plate, and let the front edge of the brace extend just beyond the rounded corner. Use countersunk screws to clamp the joint while the glue dries, then leave the screws in place to reinforce the joint. When the glue is dry, plane or sand the front surface of the brace round to match the corner of the plate. Then glue a leg to the brace and plywood plate; again use countersunk wood screws and leave them in place for reinforcement.

The side brace is so steep that fitting it is a cut-and-try procedure. It's cut from $1^{1}/_{2}$ by $1^{1}/_{2}$-inch stock. Cut the 20-degree angle first, and hold it against your squared miter to make the 70-degree cut. Start out a little too long and trim it down until it fits. Let the top extend above the leg and the front extend beyond the forward edge of the plate. Cut the excess off after the glue is dry. Leave $^{3}/_{4}$ inch between the bottom edge of the brace and the bolt hole near it; you need that much room for the wing nut to turn. Clamp the glue joint with wood screws and leave the screws in place to reinforce the joint.

Drill the remaining eight bolt holes in the plates with a $^{5}/_{16}$-inch drill to start with. The photo the bottom of the platform (at the top of the next page) shows the location of the bolt holes. Clamp the plates in place and use them for templates to drill $^{5}/_{16}$-inch bolt holes through the platform. The six bolt holes on the perimeter of the platform are okay, but the four holes in the center (the holes for the inside edges of the right side legs) need to be countersunk. If not, they will interfere with the rifle rest in use, and with the legs when they are strapped to the top surface of the platform for carrying. Countersink them just enough to clear the rounded heads of the carriage bolts—about $^{1}/_{8}$ inch. I used a $^{1}/_{2}$-inch

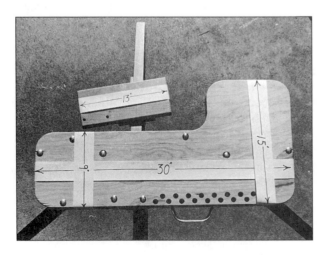

**Left:** *Top view of the assembled shooting bench. Note that the seat is offset to the rear and twisted slightly forward. The series of holes is used for holding ammunition.*

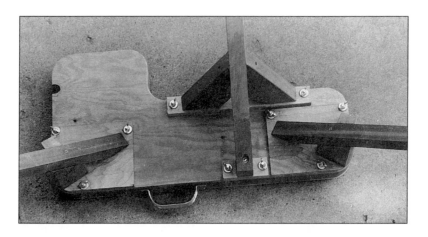

**Above:** *Bottom view of the assembled shooting bench showing the legs assembled to the plates and the plates bolted to the platform with wing nuts. The carrying handle is shown on the long edge.*

flat "spade" bit for the purpose. The tip of a spade bit needs to engage wood or it won't rotate about center, so I used a 2 ½-inch long piece of ⁵/₁₆-inch dowel pushed up into the bolt hole to engage the spade drill tip. This dowel can be reused for the other three holes.

Nine of the bolts should be 3 ½ inches long; the other is 4 ½ inches. Use the longer bolt to hold the smaller plate on the stool leg in place. It will also be used to hold the stool when carrying the bench. Glue the ten carriage bolts in place so they won't fall out and get lost. First, set them with a hammer, then drive then them back out about a half inch. Apply epoxy resin glue to the underside of the heads and reseat them. This way you won't get epoxy on the threads where it will interfere with the wing nuts. When the epoxy has set, try setting the plates over the bolts. If some of the holes don't line up, enlarge them with the next size larger drill. Washers can also get lost; glue them to the plates, but take the plates off the bolts first. You don't want epoxy glue on the threads. If you do get epoxy set up where you don't want it, heat it with a propane torch until it melts and brush it off.

With the carriage bolts in place, you can see where you want the ammunition holes to be. None should be closer than 1 inch to a bolt head, and don't get them in the way of the rifle rest, either. You can stagger them to get more holes in a limited space, but keep them all in the perimeter spacer. If you're using magnum (belted) cases, the holes need to be a little larger than ½ inch. I used a ⁹/₁₆-inch spade bit. A ½-inch hole is large enough for all standard cases.

I made the seat (stool top) by gluing two 2x4s together; mine is 5½ by 13 inches, but it can be any size you want. Note in the top view (see photo) that the seat is twisted 8 degrees toward the front. This leaves the shooter facing slightly forward, a more comfortable shooting position. The seat is also offset 1½ inches to the rear, which moves the shooter back a little so there is more room for the rifle rest at the front end of the platform. If you don't like this offset, just make the overall length of the platform 2 inches longer (32 inches), and center the seat on the left leg.

The stool isn't glued to the leg; that would make the bench hard to carry. It's just a friction fit with a stop on the leg to keep it from sliding down the leg. The stop is ½-inch plywood, held to the leg with wood screws. Build the stool by gluing the two ½-inch plywood stabilizing "ears" to the two 1 ½- by 1 ½-inch braces. Cut the ears 5½ inches wide and 6½ inches high; a 32-degree taper on the bottom gives a better-looking stool. There is no need to cut the front and back edges of the ears at an odd angle, but cut the ends of the braces at 82 degrees to match the front and back of the seat. When the glue is dry, glue the braces and ears to the bottom of the seat. Use a scrap of wood that the leg was cut from as a spacer between the ears to get the ears exactly spaced for a tight fit on the leg. Don't forget the 1½-inch offset if your platform is only 30 inches long, as mine is. Cut a 32-degree wedge and glue it between the ears; it holds the seat level. Assemble the bench and clamp the stool to the left leg with a C-clamp to start with. This lets you move the stool up and down on the leg until you find the most comfortable spot for it. Fasten the stool stop to the leg with wood screws; you may want to change its position later.

The stool is carried bolted to the bottom of the platform with the four 1/2-inch bolts that also fasten the smallest plate to the platform. Drill two 3/8-inch holes in the seat, near the edge, spaced to accept the two small plate bolts. A wing nut on the longer of the two bolts is used to fasten the stool in place for carrying.

Two brackets are used to hold the three legs to the top of the platform in the carry configuration. They're made of a strip of plywood 2 inches wide. Cut the short one 12 inches long, 3 inches longer than the width of the narrow portion of the platform. Cut the other 18 inches long to match the wider portion of the platform. Glue on a 1½- by 1½- by 2-inch block to each of the four ends of the plywood strips. Cut five blocks; you'll need an extra one. Add a 4-inch length of plywood at right angles to the longer strip, at each end. Put a screw eye through each short piece of plywood and into the block beneath it (see photo at the bottom of page 20). Use a pliers to open all four screw

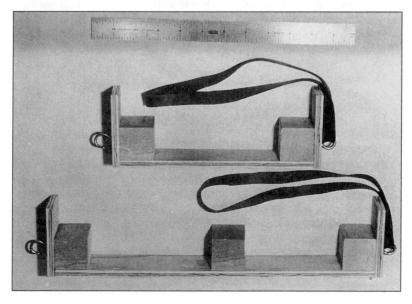

*Top:* With the shooting bench in the carrying configuration, the three legs are clamped to the top of the platform with plywood brackets. *Bottom:* These plywood brackets are used to clamp the legs to the platform for carrying.

eyes. Cut two "rubber bands" from a discarded tire inner tube about a half inch wide and fasten one into a screw eye on each bracket by closing the eye. Bend both closed eyes flat if you will want to stand the bench in its carry configuration on its edge. If you can't find an old inner tube, you may be able to make a substitute from a length of light rope and several heavy rubber bands.

Use the brackets by laying the three legs sideways on the top of the platform and "clamping" the brackets over them with the rubber bands. Place the bent-over eyes on the bottom if you want to stand the carry configuration on edge. Note that the shorter bracket holds the legs close together, but the longer bracket, over the wider portion of platform, does not. Correct this problem by gluing the extra block to the underside of the 2-inch plywood strip where it will hold the three legs together. I find this system balances best with the double plate at the large end of the platform, and a single plate at each end (see photo). But if you want to stand it on edge, put the double plate at the narrow end with the longer plate down, so it can contact the ground. Both smaller plates go to the other end.

With the stool and all three legs clamped in place for carrying, find the balance point along the long edge. Fasten the carrying handle there. I used a large "barn door" handle. You can make a wooden one if you want to save a couple of bucks. ★

# 7.

# Building A Recoil-Absorbing Gun Rest

*Here's a simple and inexpensive fixture you can build to take the kick out of testing the rifles you build and repair.*

by *Walt Netzel*

Does shooting from a bench kick you around just like you were shooting prone? Does sighting-in develop a flinch that lasts all season? Or does it just hurt to shoot from a bench? If so, you may need to replace your sand bags with a recoil-absorbing gun rest.

A recoil-absorbing gun rest is easy to build. All you need is a short length of 2x4, a few scraps of plywood, and a few dollars worth of hardware.

## How to Build It

Building the recoil-absorbing gun rest is simple. Both pieces of the base are cut from a length of 2x4. The front crosspiece is $1^5/8$ x 2 x 13 inches, with a leg hole $3/4$ inch from each end. The longitudinal piece is $1^5/8$ x $2^1/4$ x 23 inches, with a leg hole 7 inches from the rear end. The two crosspieces are held together with a 4- by 6-inch plate on both the top and bottom.

The top plate serves as the bottom of the weight box, which is 6 inches high. I cut both plates and the pieces of the box from $1/2$-inch plywood. I made the two "ears" that hold the rear end of the stock from $3/8$-inch plywood, but $1/2$-inch plywood will do. The padded front forearm support, mounted on top of the weight box, is cut from a short length of 2x4. It's padded with 3/8 inches of closed-cell plastic foam I cut from the end of a sleeping pad.

All three legs are $4^1/2$- x $3/8$-inch carriage bolts. The rounded head of a carriage bolt makes a good leg bottom; it can slide over the bench top without hanging up on a rough spot. It also allows the rear leg to rotate freely. Drill the holes for the leg bolts just a little larger than $3/8$

*Above:* By effectively tripling the mass of the gun, the recoil-absorbing gun rest reduces recoil energy to one-third the figure of the rifle alone.

inch, and countersink the bottom ends deep enough to accept a ³/₈-inch nut sunk half way in. Countersink the top of the rear leg hole, too. Turn the crosspieces up side down, and glue a nut into each countersink using epoxy resin glue. It's a good idea to screw a bolt into each nut and let it hang down through the hole while you're gluing the nut; that helps to keep the nut lined up. Be sure to oil the bolt threads beforehand; you don't want to glue the bolt in if any epoxy gets on it.

When the epoxy has set, turn the crosspieces right side up, and glue a 3/8-inch washer to the top of the front leg holes. A wing nut will bear on this washer to hold the front legs steady. The lengths of the front legs are adjusted to correct any cant in the table and to set the gun rest level.

Run a bolt up through the rear nut and leg hole and screw another nut down on the bolt until it makes contact with the countersunk wood. Tighten the nut enough allow the bolt to turn with some resistance and glue it in place. The bolt should run through both nuts and turn with light resistance.

The rear bolt is used to adjust the elevation when shooting. It is turned with the left hand if you're right-handed, and will probably need a collar to make it easier to turn. I made the collar with a 2-inch hole saw from a scrap of ³/₄-inch plywood. It's a disk that's 1⁷/₈ by ³/₄ inch, with a ³/₈-inch hole in the center. Glue it to the rear bolt about ¹/₈ inch from the head. You don't really need a round collar, it can be any size or shape.

# How It Works

The recoil-absorbing gun rest works because it's heavy—18 pounds. The weight of the gun rest is effectively added to the weight of the gun. This reduces the recoil to one-third of its original value.

We can calculate a gun's kinetic or recoil energy if we know its weight and velocity with the formula: $E = \frac{1}{2}MV^2$. For our purposes, we'll call that Formula 1. In this formula, $E$ = recoil energy of the gun in foot-pounds; $M$ = mass of the gun measured in slugs; and $V$ = velocity in feet per second.

A slug is a unit of mass that weighs 32.2 pounds at sea level. Therefore, you can easily find the mass of an object in slugs by dividing its weight in pounds by 32.2.

To find the velocity of the gun, we need to use Newton's Second Law of Motion. Basically, Newton's Second Law says that the momentum of the ejecta equals the momentum of the gun. (Momentum of Ejecta = Momentum of Gun.) Momentum, of course, is the product of mass times velocity. This brings us to what we'll call Formula 2, which is expressed as: $(M_b \times V_b) + (M_g \times V_g) = M \times V$. In this formula, $M_b$ = mass of bullet; $M_g$ = mass of gases; $V_b$ = velocity of bullet; and $V_g$ = velocity of gases.

Let's assume the bullet weighs 180 grains, has a velocity of 3,000 fps, and the powder charge weighs 60 grains. (7,000 grains equals one pound.) Since the powder burns without the addition of oxygen, the exiting hot gases also weigh 60 grains. We can estimate the average gas velocity to be 9,000 fps since it usually is about three times faster than the bullet. Therefore, $M_b$ = 180 x 1/7,000 x 1/32.2 = 0.000799 slugs; and $M_g$ = 60 x 1/7,000 x 1/32.2 = 0.000266 slugs.

Solving Formula 2, we find that 0.000799 x 3,000 = 2.40; and 0.000266 x 9,000 = 2.40; so M x V = 2.40 + 2.40 = 4.80 Slug-fps, the gun momentum. (Note that the gases produced as much momentum as the bullet. Muzzle brakes can deflect some of this gas sideways, thus reducing the effective velocity of the gas.)

Next, to find the gun's mass, divide the weight in pounds by 32.2. In our example here, M = 9/32.2 = 0.2795 slugs. To find the gun's velocity, we divide the momentum by the mass: V = 4.80/0.2795 = 17.17 fps.

Now, to find the gun's kinetic (recoil) energy, we return to Formula 1, which says that $E = \frac{1}{2}MV^2$. In this case, E = ½ x 0.2795 x 17.17 x 17.17 = 41.22 foot pounds.

If we triple the weight of the gun to 27 pounds, we increase the mass to 0.8385 slugs, but the momentum stays the same. Recalculating the velocity, we find that V = 4.80/0.8385 = 5.72 Now we can recalculate the kinetic energy with Formula 1, with the result that E= ½ x 0.8385 x 5.72 x 5.72 = 13.74 ft. lbs. This shows that recoil energy had been reduced to one-third of its original value.

We can also use Formula 1 to calculate the bullet's kinetic energy: $E_b = \frac{1}{2}M_b V_b^2$; or $E_b = $ ½ x 0.000799 x 3,000 x 3,000 = 3,954 ft. lbs.

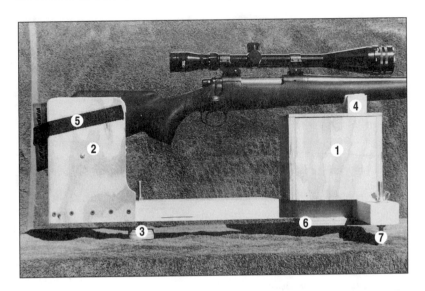

**Above:** *The right-hand side of gun rest shows the weight box (1), the right "ear" (2), the adjustable rear leg collar (3), the padded front rest (4), the nylon restraining strap (5), the lower plate (6), and the front leg (7).*

The "ears" at the rear of the rest support a strap that transfers the recoil of the rifle to the rest. I used a nylon strap and glued it to the outside of the ears with epoxy glue. It doesn't need to be nylon, but it must be securely fastened to the plywood or it will pull loose. Note how the strap slopes downward across the right ear, crosses the butt pad at the center, and continues to slope downward across the left ear. The shape of the ears is somewhat dependent on the shape of your stock. If you're right-handed, the right ear should be about as high as the comb, but not above it when both the rifle and the rest are level. The left ear should be clear of the cheek piece and extend half-way up the stock.

The toe of the stock is supported by a 3/16-inch stove bolt that goes through both ears. It's padded with a short length of rubber tubing. I didn't use a nut on the stove bolt; I just tapped the plywood ear on the left side to receive it.

Both ears need to be padded on the inside to keep the stock from touching plywood. I used closed-cell plastic foam for padding, but any soft material would work equally well. If you have a problem with the rifle canting when you're shooting off a bench, you can pad the right ear to contact the stock only at the top and bottom to prevent any rotation.

Padding, both front and rear, doesn't have to be closed-cell foam. Another idea is to use a discarded auto inner tube. Cut pads to the desired size, and build them up about six layers thick. They can be glued with contact cement. Be sure to clean all the talc off the neoprene before you start to glue. Another idea is to use a discarded bicycle inner tube. Cut it a little longer than needed; fill it half full of sand; bend the ends over; and fasten it in place with wood screws. Contact cement

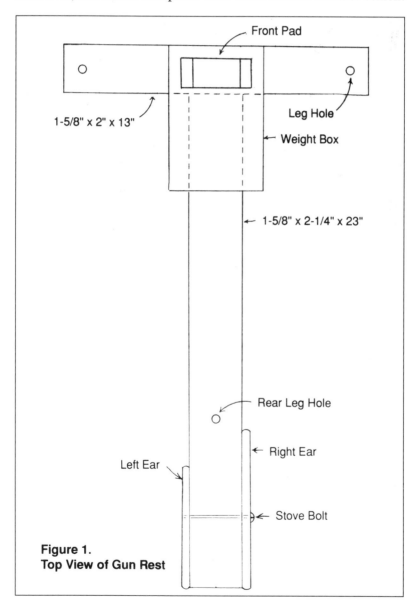

**Figure 1.**
**Top View of Gun Rest**

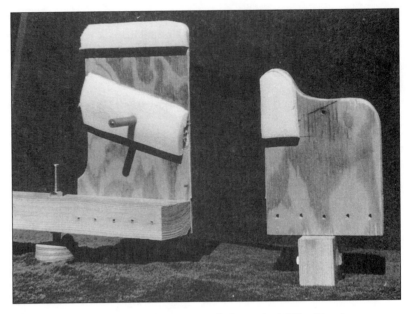

*Above: In this left-side view of the rear end of rest, the left "ear" has been re-moved and set to the side to show the padding on the inside of both ears.*

will also help hold it in place. If nothing else is available, try cutting up a kitchen sponge for padding.

To bring the weight of the rest up to 18 pounds, I filled the weight box with about 10 pounds of wheel weights and added enough sand to completely fill the box. The sand is added to hold the wheel weights in place. If the weights are allowed to move during recoil, they won't do much to absorb the shock. It may be a good idea to contain the sand and wheel weights in a plastic zip-lock storage bag. This will help to keep sand from leaking out of the box. I also fastened the box top in place with wood screws.

If you need a handle to carry this gun-rest, glue a 19-inch-long nylon strap to the sides of the weight box at the center of gravity. Leave enough slack at the top for hand room. It won't interfere with shooting.    ★

# 8.

# Do-It-Yourself Safety for Smith & Wesson Revolvers

*This easy-to-make safety won't make your revolver childproof, but it could prevent it from being turned against you.*

*by Chip Todd*

Most of my family's revolvers have manual safeties on them, and we've become so accustomed to them that we don't think of them as unusual anymore. I added this feature to them after seeing one on a Los Angeles policeman's service revolver. This simple and unobtrusive safety is a modification you can make yourself. And there are no visible new parts.

This revolver safety was originally invented to give a policeman an extra 5 to 10 seconds to draw his backup weapon if his duty handgun was taken by surprise or force. These precious seconds could mean the difference between life and death for the law-enforcement officer. Please note that I do not claim that this safety is effective against a child's curious fingers, so please don't read this into my description. Children present another problem; I feel that something solid—a locking mechanism of some type—must be employed to childproof a handgun.

Many years ago, a father-and-son gunsmithing team from Inglewood, California, dreamed up and patented a conversion kit for this revolver safety. (I can no longer find a current address for their company, Armament Safety International.) I had my first one installed by them, and bought several of their kits. Eventually, I devised the method described here, which, in my opinion, is a better and less-expensive way to do the same thing.

This safety works by blocking the rearward movement of the cylinder bolt. The bolt has a dogleg foot in the rear that blocks the hammer's rearward travel unless the cylinder is closed. The trigger is captured by the hammer's double-action sear, so neither can travel rear-

63

*Right: This Smith & Wesson Model 19 is shown with the thumbpiece in the safety position (arrow). Thumb pressure downward takes the gun out of the safe position. The safety blocks both the hammer and the trigger from functioning.*

ward. The thumbpiece, when rotated up to catch in the notch in its slot, retains the bolt in its forward position by wedging into the notch. Thumb pressure, downward on the thumbpiece, rotates it out of the notch, allowing the bolt to be pushed back by the cylinder's center pin, as it normally does.

The slight upward cant of the thumbpiece isn't noticeable when one isn't looking for it. I have passed my revolver around a roomful of gunsmithing students without anyone being able to tell why the gun was locked up. Of course, if you know about the safety, you'll notice the slightly canted thumbpiece.

The Armament Safety kit came with a new, longer stud, longer stainless-steel thumbpiece nut, a wave washer, a template, and a $60 price tag. As this was rather steep, I made enough modifications and improvements to their idea to feel comfortable (and legal) about doing it my way. I also thought that the stainless thumbpiece nut was likely to give away the presence of the safety on blued guns.

## The Commercial System

To install the Armament Safety version, the cylinder-bolt stud must be drilled out from the rear using a $3/32$-inch drill bit. This drilling must be in the center of the stud or the location of the new stud will be off and may not allow the thumbpiece to set properly. The hole must be tapped to 4-48 threads for the stepped stud supplied in the kit. After cleaning all the tapping fluid from the cylinder bolt, the new stud is installed with some thread-locking compound. Armament Safety suggests staking the stud in, as the safety was designed for police use and they like "positive" installations.

After the stud is installed, the notch in the frame and the thumbpiece modification are done, and the stud length sometimes needs filing to fit. The cylinder bolt is reinstalled and the gun reassembled. Then, the thumbpiece is dropped onto the new stud, the wave washer follows it, and the nut is screwed on. The nut is designed to be bottomed out against the top of the new stud, and if it doesn't, the stud must be filed to length.

This conversion irrevocably changes the cylinder bolt and the thumbpiece. While the thumbpiece is easy to replace, the cylinder bolt is expensive and may have to be fitted. It would be possible to put a small roll pin in the right place on the thumbpiece and file the stud of the bolt shorter, but this is would make it hard to go back to a safety system.

## Doing It My Way

One of the nicest things about doing the conversion my way, is that the changes don't show and the firearm can be put back into original form with only replacement of the thumbpiece. The thumbpiece completely covers the small notch cut into the thumbpiece's slot in the receiver, so the gun appears completely original. Armament Safety's method of replacing the thumbpiece's stud requires the purchase of another part to return the gun to original looks. Armament Safety's conversion called for removing the thumbpiece stud and tapping the

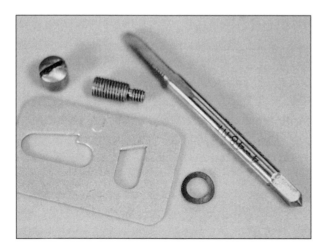

*Left: The Armament Safety kit consists of a thumbpiece stud, wave washer, scribing template, and longer thumbpiece nut. The 4-48 tap shown at the right is not included in the $60 price.*

*Right: The only new components needed for the do-it-yourself safety are the ball bearing (or lead shot), and the single coil of a spring, both shown in the center of the photo.*

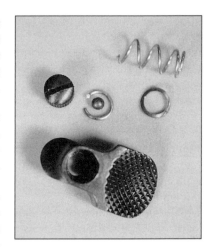

hole to 4-48 threads to accept the replacement stud. They staked in the stud, but with such good thread-locking compounds available, I feel that staking is not necessary.

The parts changed by my method are the cylinder bolt, the receiver, and thumbpiece. I also add a #8 lead shot and either a wave washer or one coil of a compression spring. This cuts the cost of doing this conversion to about a penny, and the whole process should only take about a half-hour the first time, and less than 15 minutes after that. Part of this time is spent checking out the cylinder-lock plunger for length. For some reason, S&W often puts an overlength one in. No harm is done by this, but it makes disassembly and reassembly somewhat more troublesome. We'll go into that later.

The original design called for a longer cylinder-bolt stud so that the thumbpiece nut could be constrained from tightening upon the thumbpiece. This was necessary so that the thumbpiece could be rotated slightly to catch the notch in the top of the slot in the frame. The original kit accomplished this by supplying a longer stud and a longer (deeper) thumbpiece nut. Personally, I think these parts were necessary only to justify the rather steep price of the kit. In my system, the lead shot acts as a spacer which stops the thumbpiece nut from tightening the thumbpiece against the cylinder bolt. The lead can be shaped and adjusted with force in tightening the nut.

If you are uncomfortable with using the lead shot—I was initially—it's pretty easy to locate the proper size steel ball bearing. (They can be found at any bearing and gasket supply store or from Brownells.) I would use a ball between .087 and .127 inch in diameter; my preference being about .093 (3/32 inch). The height is adjustable as described later. The lead shot I use most often is .087 inch in diameter. This allows me to go to a larger size shot if the receiving hole is a little deeper than I meant it to be.

The purpose of the wave washer is to add drag between the thumbpiece and the nut to keep the thumbpiece from flopping up and down out of control. This would be a dead giveaway (pun intended). You can make the wave washer yourself, although it is not really worth the effort. The perfect wave washer is .225 OD x .160 ID x .013 thick x .050 total height. As it isn't worth the time hunting a source, I use one coil of a compression spring which has a .210 OD and is made of .025 diameter wire. The coil is cut off with a Dremel rotary tool using a thin cutoff wheel. This tool is also used to smooth off the ends of the wire perpendicular to the "bore." This is so that it will slide on the contacted surfaces like the wave washer would do. If it digs in, it might loosen the thumbpiece nut.

The cylinder bolt will need a hole center-drilled into the end of the stud; the frame will need a small notch filed into the top of its slot; and the thumbpiece will need the lug (the portion which sticks into the slot in the frame) reshaped with a file. This can also be done on a mill, although it is less trouble to cut the metal away with a file than it is to put the piece in the mill at the right angle.

## The Installation Process

Disassemble the revolver by taking the grips off, remove the sideplate screws, and tap the right side of the gripframe with a soft hammer. Inertia will jolt the sideplate off, so be ready to catch it. I do the tapping with the firearm held right-side-up in my left hand and tap with the hammer in my right hand. My left thumb and middle finger are extended upward to trap the sideplate and keep it from falling. I also do this over a soft pad, as even Ozzie Smith has dropped an easy catch before. Remove the mainspring by loosening the tension screw on the front of the gripframe and slide it from the frame. Using a pick or some-

**Left:** The finished slot shows the countersunk stud and the location of the notch. The template isn't needed, as the notch is described in the text.

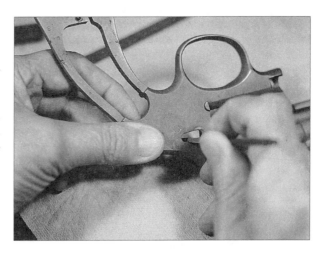

*Right: Cut the notch for the safety using a triangular needle file. The angle of the file causes a slight backward slant to the rear of the notch. This helps give a firm capture in the safe position.*

thing small and stiff, pry the rebound block and rebound spring from the receiver and remove the hammer and trigger.

Now remove the thumbpiece nut and thumbpiece, and then push the cylinder bolt rearward and lift up on the front of it. It should be able to be taken out like this. If the front of the bolt won't clear the hole through the breech face, its plunger is too long. This will call for returning the bolt forward and lifting the rear of the bolt. Take care to capture the plunger and spring which will shoot out of the bolt when it clears the rear of the frame inlet.

At this time, I would fit the plunger to the bolt so that the bolt can be removed and replaced in the intended fashion. This calls for grinding the nose of the plunger off until it fits into the bolt with its spring, and can be pushed flush with the rear of the bolt. Be sure to buff off the sharp edges caused by the grinding, although leaving them on won't really hurt the frame. (There are some things you should do just for neatness and self-satisfaction.)

Finish the disassembly of the gun by removing the cylinder and crane assembly, and the cylinder lock and its spring. This will allow you to properly clean away all grit produced by the filing operation. I keep the cylinder and crane assembly together, as they are used to check the frame's notch depth before reassembling the handgun.

My next step is to place the bolt in a vise, preferably in a mill, although it can be done on a drill press or by hand drill. Now start a center drill in the center of the stud. The size of center drill I use is a #1 with a .050-inch nose and a 1/8-inch diameter shank. Drill until the countersink portion of the drill cuts to where the countersunk hole in the stud is about the same diameter as the shot you are going to use. Stop there, for now.

The notch in the frame is done on the top of the notch, about .375 inch back from the front of the slot and not more than about .050 inch high. If the notch is too tall, it will show when the thumbpiece is in place, spoiling the looks and defeating the purpose (secrecy). Of course, be careful, as it is easy to slip and drag the scribe across the gun's nice bluing. If you are the extra-cautious type, the rearward location of the notch can be marked inside the thumbpiece notch and the depth of the notch tried as you file. This is the way I do this particular part of the job, after having done quite a few.

I cut the notch with a small triangular file so I can achieve a slight back angle (about 10 degrees) to the notch, which aids the tiny spring in the cylinder bolt. If this slight back angle is made, the thumbpiece actually has to be ramped slightly forward when it is pushed down to be released. This gives a more positive feel to the safety, and allows the cylinder-bolt spring to push the thumbpiece further into the locked position, aiding the engagement. Before reassembling the gun, the location of the notch can be tested by reinstalling the cylinder and crane, and trying the safe position's feel.

I always scribe the intended cut to the thumbpiece, since it is done on the inside of the part and is to be filed anyway. It's good to start out with the mark about .350 inch at the top and .280 inch at the bottom, about a 17-degree angle, and file forward until the thumbpiece proves itself when trying it with the cylinder/crane assembly temporarily installed. It is amazing how soft the metal of the thumbpiece is. I tried hardening it once, but that made it hard to cold-blue. Later, I realized that the "sear and notch" of this safety didn't operate under the pressure that the gun's regular sear did, so there wasn't any measurable wear.

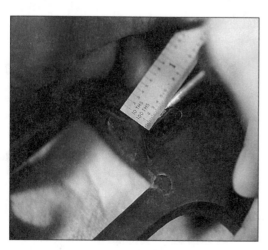

The aforementioned filing is easily done with a standard mill-cut bastard file, and there is no need to worry about scratching the backside of the thumbpiece, as it is out of

*Left:* You can scribe the pattern by the cylinder bolt's slot, but the only part of the scribing which is really necessary is the rear limit scratch.

view and will be cold-blued when finished. Be sure to file the part of the boss you want removed all the way down to the main portion of the thumbpiece, or it might not catch reliably in the notch. When the filing is all done and the piece has proven to catch the notch, reblue it with your favorite cold-bluing compound. I usually use Brownells Ox-pho-Blue, although T4 is also quite good. And Birchwood Casey makes a couple of good bluing pastes called Ultra-Blue and Super-Blue.

If the thumbpiece drags on the side of the receiver, it will need to be shimmed up, or it will leave telltale scratches on the bluing. These scratches will be unsightly and will give the safety away. Small shim washers can be made from brass shim stock or a small washer that has been filed to the proper thickness. I would have a minimum of .020 inch between the frame and the thumbpiece throughout its whole travel. In some cases, I have found that the wave washer (or spring coil) that I planned to use between the thumbpiece and the cylinder bolt was best placed over the bolt stud before the thumbpiece was put on. This gave the same overall effect, but had the additional duty of keeping the thumbpiece off of the bluing. You'll have to make up your own mind on where to put this wave washer/spring coil.

After all this work, the receiver must be thoroughly cleaned so that any grit from filing and stoning is washed out of the inside cavity. I feel good about introducing some fresh lubricant into any gun when it is apart, anyway. I usually remove the cylinder lock and spring to make sure that no grit has found its way into the spring recess. The cylinder bolt's groove in the receiver is another likely place for grit to accumulate.

## Conclusion

The reassembly of the revolver is done in the reverse, and there should be no tricks needed. There should be one or more of the fine

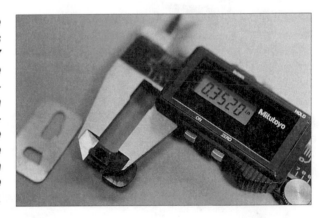

**Right:** File the thumb-piece's boss to 17 degrees and the overall dimensions stated in the text. Calipers show the length of the boss is within .002 inch of the nominal .350.

assembly/disassembly books in every gunsmith's library, so, you should acquire one if you don't have one. You will find lots of useful information you can use when friends ask you to fiddle with their guns, and they will.

If the work was done carefully, there should be no sign that any work has been done to this revolver. Therefore, the value of the firearm should have gone up, if it has changed at all. If a potential buyer isn't thrilled with the safety, then I would either install another stock thumbpiece, or give him a new thumbpiece along with instructions for undoing the thumbpiece nut, removing the lead shot and wave washer, and installing the new thumbpiece. He would then have a stock S&W, again.

Finally, if I were to sell one of my revolvers with this safety on it, I would make sure that I told the buyer to practice with the gun enough so that taking the safety off was a reflex action. By no means is this safety to be considered in the same light as a trigger-locking device or other more secure device. It was only designed to hamper the quick use by someone who wasn't familiar with the gun. ★

# 9.

# Make a Forearm Brace For the Model 21

*This Winchester's forearm iron can shift during recoil, eventually causing damage. The recoil abutment eliminates the problem.*

*by Dennis A. Wood*

We often hear or read about the high-quality craftsmanship done by the old-time gunmakers—as if they had some mystical way of doing things. Truth be known, most of those people were paid very little, and time didn't mean much as long as the job was done right and deadlines were met. The point I'm trying to make is that, back in the "good old days," guns weren't very expensive by today's standards, and the quality was by no means consistent. That's primarily because piecework rates were low, and there were no high-output machines that cost millions of dollars.

So what does that have to do with Winchester Model 21 forearms? The inletting of the forearm iron on these forearms was done by hand back then, and, to the credit of those who did it well, it was no easy task. But when I look over these shotguns, I find that the skills of the individuals doing the inletting of the forearm iron range from excellent to quite poor.

## Forearm Styles

The Winchester Model 21 has always been pricey for a side-by-side shotgun. Even back when they were first introduced, there were other shotguns that could be had for one-third or one-fourth the price. With today's inflated currency, it's common to see a Model 21 Winchester selling for $3,000 or more.

The Model 21 was available for just about any sport or game of the day. Trap, skeet, and upland hunting versions were produced; and, for the waterfowler, a 32-inch barreled Magnum 12 gauge was offered.

73

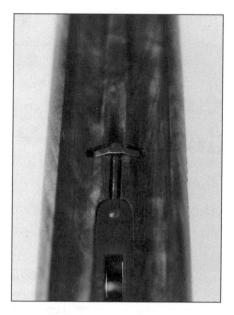

**Above:** *Around 1950, Winchester added the recoil abutment as a standard feature.*

Along with the different barrel lengths, gauges, and choke sizes, different forearms were designed to accommodate the comfort of the off hand by helping the shotgun to swing toward the target. Represented here are three types of forearm: a beavertail field-grade style, skeet style, and the trap style—all for the 12 gauge.

The field-grade style is slimmer in width and doesn't reach up along the sides of the barrel quite so drastically. The skeet style is wider and flatter than the field version, and reaches up the barrels sides a little farther. The trap style is slimmer than the skeet style but the side walls of the forearm reach up and wrap around the barrels slightly more. All of these styles have a purpose, and that is to prevent the off hand from getting hot during a shooting session. Trap forearms protect the off hand from heat when the barrels get hot during doubles shooting events. A field-grade forearm is used for carrying the shotgun and steadying the swing on occasional game, so they don't normally come up as high along the sides. (If the barrels get too hot on your field gun, let me know where you are hunting; that's just too much shooting for one man to handle, and I'd be more than willing to help you out.)

There were factory drawings with targeted dimensions for each of the different forearm styles. The people shaping these different forearms were paid on a piecework basis, so you will see slight discrepancies between like variations. Even though the factory had these size specifications for each style variation, they were rarely clones of one another.

The Model 21 is what can be considered a premium-grade shotgun for the most part. Along with the "deluxe" title goes the look and cosmetics of a high-grade shotgun. This means that the wood is usually of a fancier grade, most often nicely grained and figured American walnut. When we get into the more appealing looking wood, grain, figure and color are a big factor.

To maintain the sleek, clean lines that the Model 21 is noted for, the forearm cannot look "clubby." Nevertheless, a thin forearm with swirling grain can create problems.

## What's the Brace For?

When areas in a stock or forearm become thin from inletting, especially in open-grained wood such as American walnut, cracking and splitting are likely to result. Add to this the sometimes erratic grain configuration of the more desirably colored and figured wood, and recoil shock is not suffered easily.

Prior to World War II, the forearm brace—called a "forearm recoil abutment" by Winchester—is not seen in forearms. Factory drawings of around 1947 show inletting in the fore-arm for the brace, and they became standard procedure after about 1950. This is not to say that the brace won't show up on forearms made prior to 1947, as undoubtedly there were many that were sent back to the factory to correct the inevitable cracks or splits.

There are two styles of bracing that can be found on these forearms. The most obvious attempt will be seen at the front of the forearm iron. The idea involved with this process required inletting of a blued steel plate or "abutment," with a small screw going through it and then threaded into the front end of the

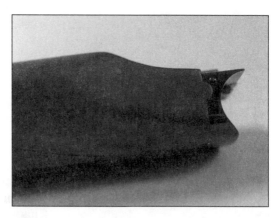

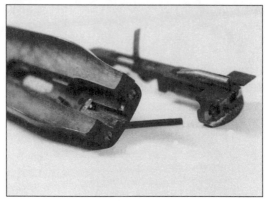

*Top:* The convex radius in the forearm pivot shoe makes for a tough inletting job. *Bottom:* The other method of correction left the rear of the forearm weaker.

forearm iron. A more obscure attempt had a screw going through the rear face of the forearm iron pivot shoe, and threaded into a brace underneath the forearm iron. This second type of bracing really bothers me, because of the further thinning of the forearm wood when cutting relief for the brace and screw. If added support was the intent, then why remove more wood, which could cause cracks rather than prevent them?

Another attempt to support the rear face of the forearm was the addi-

tion of a $1/4$-inch ebony block, wood-screwed in place. Yes, ebony is harder than walnut, and has a higher shock resistance; but when you are dealing with the endgrain of a stock, you normally have a very strong surface. Shock will find the path of least resistance and, wherever longitudinal grain is found in a thin area, a crack or split is sure to result.

Because of the small concave radius in the front of the forearm shoe, and the problems with inletting this radius and the 90-degree inletting for the front of the forearm iron, there are going to be areas where the wood-to-metal fit will not be as good as it should be. This mismatch in fit allows

*Top:* A forearm abutment and draw screw were supposed to correct the cracking problem. *Center:* Drill the end of the forearm iron and tap with #8-40 threads. *Bottom:* Before epoxy bedding the rear face of the forearm, fill the holes with clay and paint the area with release agent.

the forearm iron to shift fore and aft during recoil, causing minute battering which will eventually do damage. The forearm recoil abutment was designed to eliminate this problem.

## Forearm Abutment Dimensions

The owners of Winchester Model 21 shotguns are people who know the history of this shotgun, what they're worth, and are adamant about keeping them original. The forearm depicted here was made during the era when the folks at Winchester were adding the 1/4-inch-thick ebony support spacer at the back of the fore-

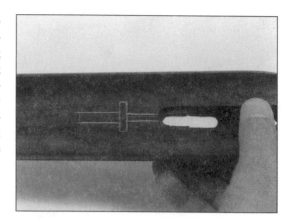

**Above left:** White lines act as a guide for the chisel cuts. **Above right:** The last cut is made to allow access for the screwdriver blade.

arm and the rear style of abutment. Predictably, this process did not prevent an inertia shock crack from developing at the back of the forearm. I did my best to talk the owner into having the forearm iron epoxy bedded into the forearm, explaining that the iron would then fit in the wood like a duck's foot in mud. The only area he would allow to be epoxied was the back face of the forearm and in the area that was inletted for the rear draw screw. He then wanted the forward style of abutment installed so that it would resemble what was done at the Winchester factory.

The original abutments appear to be cut out of flat steel stock with a stamping die. The one I made was out of 1/8-inch cold rolled steel,

*Left: A strip of cellophane tape around the edge of the stock will prevent the epoxy from sticking to the outside of the stock.*

though stainless steel is better yet. (With stainless steel there is less likelihood of the abutment rusting, but it's hard to blue the part.) Start with a piece of stock $^1/_8$ thick by $^3/_4$ by $^1/_2$ inch, with the $^3/_4$ dimension being the width (see Figure 1). From the bottom of the little plate of steel, center punch a dimple on an intersect line $^3/_8$-inch from either side and $^7/_{32}$ inch up from the bottom. Drill a through hole in the dimple with a #19 twist drill. Then scribe a line across the $^3/_4$-inch width 0.415 inch from the bottom. Scribe another line across the $^3/_4$-inch width 0.240 inch from the bottom. Using a protractor set at 20 degrees, scribe a line from each edge of the bottom scribed line to the top scribed line. Mill or file the excess off the plate and remove any burrs.

A 1-inch-long fillister-head screw with #8-40 threads running about $^1/_2$ inch will be used for anchoring. Drill a #28 hole into the end of the forearm iron, and tap the hole for #8-40. If this hole is run into the threaded area for the front hold-down screw, it would be wise to run a tap into the hold-down hole to clean up any burrs created there.

## Inletting the Forearm

There are three inletting cuts that will need to be made in the forearm for the recoil abutment.

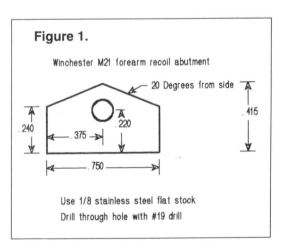

**Figure 1.**

Winchester M21 forearm recoil abutment

20 Degrees from side

.240

.375

.220

.415

.750

Use 1/8 stainless steel flat stock
Drill through hole with #19 drill

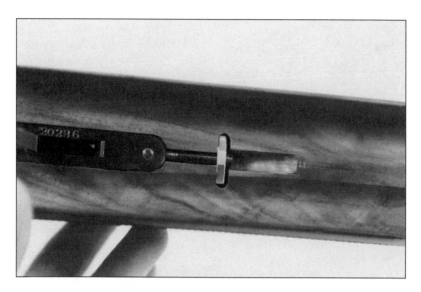

**Above:** *The end result is a job much the same—though not exactly the same—as Winchester did it 50 years ago.*

These cuts can be made in a milling machine or they can be done with hand chisels. For simplicity's sake, it's best to pencil in the cuts with a white lead pencil or whatever makes a good outline to guide you. The relief cut just in front of the forearm iron is a $^3/_{16}$-inch-wide by $^3/_4$-inch-long trough that provides clearance for the draw screw. The depth of this inletting should go to the same depth as that for the forearm iron. If this is done with hand chisels, it's best to cut the sides first to help eliminate any splintering of the wood at these edges.

The crosscut for the abutment plate is $^3/_{16}$-inch wide and 1 inch in length. This cut is made to a depth of $^1/_2$-inch from the top of the center area that fits against the under rib in the barrels. The last longitudinal cut is $^1/_4$-inch wide and about 1 inch long. This cut angles down from the front toward the bottom of the abutment plate. This is an access clearance cut so that a screwdriver blade can get to the draw screw.

Once all the cuts are made, try a dry fit of the abutment plate to see if any more wood needs to be removed. When satisfied that everything fits as it should, a couple of coats of stock finish on the exposed wood is the next step.

Whenever possible, it's always best to bed these parts in epoxy so they fit exactly. Of course, if the owner insists that you do it the same way that it was done at Winchester, you can do it that way. ★

# 10.

# How To Get Started
# In Gunstock Carving

*Adding custom woodwork touches to stocks
beautifies and personalizes firearms. Here
are the implements you need.*

*By Philip R. Eck*

**M**any times over the years I've heard the words, "You carved these gunstocks with those tools?" and other stock carvers I know have heard them too. Those who view my tools appear surprised that I don't use tools that require an engineering degree to operate. One couple seemed to feel sorry I couldn't afford better. Most people expect the tools of this trade to be similar to those used by cabinetmakers, but that is not the case.

A gunstock carver's tools are chiefly a hodgepodge collection of items that have been lying around for years and others that were resurrected from a scrap pile. These were then altered for this type of carving. My tools are definitely not fancy or expensive. Even when done professionally, stock carving can be undertaken with little more than pocket money for basic essentials. Flea markets and yard sales offer excellent opportunities for picking up tools and essentials that can be adapted for the trade.

## Basic Set of Tools

This list of tools is by no means absolute, and you do not need to duplicate all of them unless you intend to do a large amount of carving. A sizable number of well-carved stocks have proved these tools' value, and I am certain they will serve others as well.

I've seen carvings done with nothing but an ordinary jackknife. Most were not that well done from a professional viewpoint, but some ranged from respectable to very good. I've often wondered how much better the very good ones might have been had the carver used more tools. The goal of carving is quality workmanship; don't settle for anything

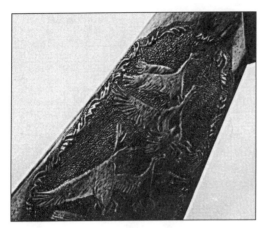

**Above:** *To add detailed carvings like this to gunstocks, you'll need specialized tools.*

less. In the descriptions that follow, I indicate which tools I feel are absolutely necessary for the beginner. If you do not know some of the items by name, familiarize yourself with them by studying the photograph of tools that accompanies this article.

## Magni-viewer

After my first attempt at stock carving, I have not made a single cut without a magni-viewer. This particular model is equipped with a replaceable, scratch-resistant 2X magnification lens. With this tool, you can trace and transfer a pattern to a stock and make intricate cuts more easily and precisely. The tool reduces eyestrain, and the lens housing blocks out everything but what you are viewing and keeps your focus on the carving. If you have exceptionally good eyesight, you may be able to make do without this item, but otherwise it is a must.

It certainly is a must if you intend to do professional work regardless of how good your eyesight might be. You can obtain this item from a number of sources, but your best bet for a quality product is a hobby shop or jeweler supply store. There are several styles available, ranging from fixed-lens to variable-power, with a range of prices to match. I prefer a fixed-lens magni-viewer with a lens housing section that can be lifted while the headband stays in place. This allows me to position the headband at another spot or angle on my forehead should it become uncomfortable during a lengthy carving session. For anyone who wears eyeglasses, a clip-on type is available at jeweler supply stores.

## X-acto Knives

Standard X-acto knifes are readily obtained at hardware stores, hobby shops, craft shops, and art supply stores. You can make do with just one of these knives, but I prefer to have at least three on hand. With three, I don't have to stop to sharpen or change a blade as often, or be disrupted while I'm working on an area that calls for complete concentration.

The knives marked C and D in the accompanying photograph have the same type of blade, but the handle of knife C is thicker in diameter. Knife D is my favorite; I use this one for the bulk of my carving. I occasionally use the other knife to break monotony and get a different feel when I'm carving for long periods of time. The smaller handle size of knife D is the size recommended if you will be using just one knife. The smaller-diameter handle will allow cuts to be at angles that the larger handle will not.

The only knife blade I use is the X-acto #16 slant-blade. It is perfect for initial parting-line cuts and does extremely well when used in chisel-like fashion to remove background wood from large areas. Take note of the blade in knife E. It too is a #16 slant-blade, altered to the shape shown. I use the D handle with this blade. I wish the blade came in this shape, but such is not the case. I used a Dremel tool fitted with a carbide disc to modify the blade. You can use a mill file, but this will take a considerable amount of time and effort. The blade's reduced size allows access for detail work in difficult areas and is particularly useful in making outline cuts in tight curved areas. It's also very good in high-

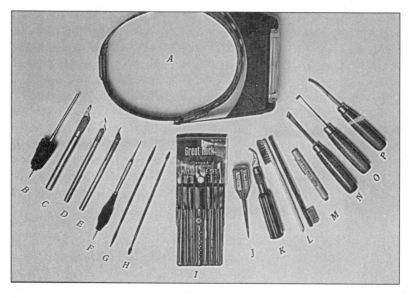

**Above:** *The basic tools you need for gunstock carving include: A, magni-viewer; B, dental tool for design transfer; C, X-acto knife with wide grip; D, X-acto knife with narrow grip; E, X-acto knife with altered blade; F, dental tool for scraping and picking small areas; G and H, file rifflers; I, mill file set; J, scratch awl; K, X-acto knife with hook-bill blade; L, toothbrushes; M, magnet; N, skewered chisel; O, straight chisel; P, bent chisel.*

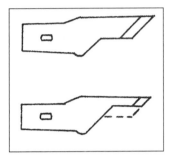

**Above**: *The X-acto #16 slant-blade can be altered to the shape shown. Use a Dremel tool fitted with a carbide disc to modify the blade. The blade's reduced size allows access for detail work in difficult areas and is particularly useful in making outline cuts in tight curved areas. It's also very good in high-detail work such as feathers.*

detail work such as feathers and facial features. Altered or unaltered, the #16 slant-blade is the gem of the entire X-acto line.

## Design Transfer Dental Tool

For transferring the design from the pattern paper to the gunstock, I use a dental tool that I modified with a mill file, removing a slight angle from the tip and forming a point. Then I smoothed the point and gave it a final polish with emery paper. This tool needs only an occasional touch-up to maintain its point. I occasionally use this tool to stipple in limited or hard-to-reach areas.

Although the tool produces a smaller stipple than is usually seen in larger accessible areas, the combination of large and small stippling blends together nicely. To do this, stipple the larger areas first with the larger stippling tool, then stipple the more confined areas with this smaller tool, allowing the smaller marks to run in with the larger stippling.

Place these smaller marks on the higher areas surrounding the larger marks; they should decrease in depth and number as they extend into the larger markings. Generally, it's only necessary to extend into the larger markings no more than $^1/_8$ inch to $^1/_4$ inch. This is best judged by appearance rather than by a set rule.

The tool's handle is about the thickness of a ball-point pen, so it can become uncomfortable to work with for any length of time. I found that wrapping the tool with masking tape gives a firm, comfortable, controlled grip during long periods of use and greatly reduces or eliminates finger cramping.

You will need this tool or something similar to transfer the design to the stock. There are other ways to transfer designs, but I have found none so precise as the puncture method. Flea markets, military surplus stores, scrap yards, and of course, dentists, are the best places to find dental tools. Your dentist might give you this tool at no cost. A similar tool, with a wooden handle, is available at ceramics and plaster craft shops. It is also easy enough to make your own tool. To do so, use a 5-inch length of $^3/_8$- or $^1/_2$-inch wooden dowel. Drill a hole in one end of the dowel about half the length of a large sewing needle and large enough in diameter to allow insertion of the needle without force. Run about 2 inches of thread through the eye of the needle, leaving an inch on each side. Dip the threaded half into epoxy or good glue, such as carpenter's glue, and insert that end into the hole in the dowel, turning the needle while you do so. Add more glue if necessary to ensure that the area around the needle is solidly filled. Wipe off any excess, and let the dowel stand overnight in an upright position. You can temporarily use tape to make certain the needle remains straight while the glue hardens. Then remove the temporary tape and trim, shape, and tape the handle as shown in the accompanying drawing. When not in use, insert the needle into a cork or like object to protect the point.

## Dental Tool for Scraping

I use a second dental tool as a pick, chisel, and scraper in areas that are very difficult to reach with ordinary tools. I used a Dremel tool to modify the cutting edge, then finished it with a stone. The final length of the blade is slightly less than $^{1}/_{32}$-inch. Although this tool can be done without, it makes carving gunstocks a lot easier, and I highly recommend that it be among those in your toolbox.

## File Rifflers

File rifflers can be purchased at shops dealing in hobby woods, exotic woods, and materials used in furniture making, as well as hobby shops and jeweler supply stores. Do

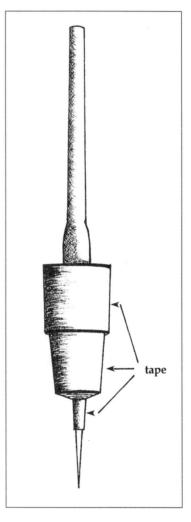

tape

**Above:** *Use a dental tool to transfer designs from pattern paper to the gunstock. The tool's handle is about the thickness of a ball-point pen, so it can become uncomfortable to work with for any length of time. Wrapping the tool with masking tape gives a firm, comfortable, controlled grip during long periods of use and greatly reduces finger cramping.*

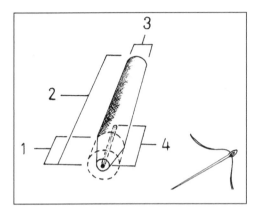

**Above**: *These are the items you need to make your own design transfer tool: a 5-inch length of ³/₈ or ¹/₂-inch wooden dowel, a large sewing needle, thread, and epoxy or other good glue.*

not confuse them with rasp rifflers, which are too harsh for use on gunstocks. Of the two shown, riffler H is the workhorse. I use it to remove tool marks, to point up design side walls, and in some instances for final shaping. Riffler G is not as suited for final shaping; I use it strictly for removing tool marks and high spots in the background. These tools are not essential, but they make gunstock carving easier and faster.

## Mill-File Set

I use mill files for the same purpose as the rifflers, but on a smaller scale. Their size and variety of shapes allow better access to the more difficult areas and help in shaping specific areas of the design. I consider a mill-file set to be a must.

## Scratch-Awl

Chances are you already have this item lying around the house somewhere. If not, you can pick one up inexpensively at a discount hardware store or a flea market. For stock use, you'll need to round off the awl's sharp point slightly, using emery paper or a mill file, so that it will take a bit of pressure for the awl to indent wood. This is a necessary tool.

## Hook-Bill Knife

The hook-bill is a type of X-acto blade that excels in the incised work common to carvings on flintlocks. Otherwise, this blade is seldom used, and it is not a necessary tool unless you intend to work on black-powder rifles such as the Pennsylvania long rifle.

## Toothbrushes

The toothbrush no doubt is used for more things other than its original purpose than any other brush made. I recommend having two toothbrushes in your tool kit: One to brush the area clean of shavings during the carving process, and the other to apply stain or remove excess wet finish after the carving is complete. So that you don't confuse the two, use toothbrushes of different colors. These are must items.

## Magnet

An ordinary magnet, although not absolutely essential, is useful to have on hand to clean up steel-wool fibers from the carving and surrounding work area.

## Assorted Carving Tools

I also own a set of six Garrett Wade carving tools sold under the name Henry Taylor. Three are shown here. They are exceptionally good tools imported from England. I bought them on a day when I felt like being nice to myself.

For their exceptional quality, they are not all that expensive, and they deserve looking into should you decide to add some special tools to your kit. Chisel N is a skew chisel. It serves the same functions as the slant-blade knife but on a much larger scale. I have found this tool to be excellent for removing large amounts of wood from background areas and have begun to use it more and more; it has really become a fa-

# Other Helpful Items

In addition to working tools, there are several materials that you should have on hand at all times. All carvers will need the items on list A, and those who will be stock-carving on a larger scale will need those on list B as well.

## List A

Steel wool (000) or (0000)
Sandpaper (fine and extra fine)
Masking tape
Tracing paper
Workbench pad
Stock protection pads
Stain (optional)
Stock finish
Combination varnish and
   lacquer remover

## List B

Chisels
Sharpening stones
   (coarse, medium, and fine)
Slip
Strop
Pantograph or Magna-Jector
Drawing pens and pencils
Assorted stains
Spray gun or finish
   application brushes
Drawing display photo albums

vorite. Chisel O is a straight chisel, and P is a bent chisel.

Each has a straight cutting edge at 90 degrees to the handle. The shank of the bent chisel curves slightly upward. This chisel is seldom used in any woodcraft profession, but it serves well in getting to areas where the shank of a straight chisel would touch wood and cause damage to that area. All three chisels are easy to work with and hold a fine cutting edge for long periods of extensive use. Though they are not necessary, I recommend them.                    ★

# 11.

# Easy Do-It-Yourself Hex Sockets

*It is easy to make Allen-head screws or hex sockets. Here's a simple method for making as good a hex socket as any you've ever seen.*

*by Chip Todd*

Hex sockets are just a round hole that have six corners broached into it. After studying the socket bottom of a bunch of Allen-head screws, I came to the conclusion that I could make them if I had a homemade broach made from some very hard material. At the lock company where I designed bank locks, the tooling shop had some hardened tooling pins which almost took diamonds to scratch, so I got some throwaway pins and worked them over on a surface grinder.

The first ones I made were put into a spin/indexer, and the flats were ground out laboriously on a surface grinder. After each pass, I would spin the pin 60 degrees, and duplicate the grind until the stone stopped throwing up sparks. I repeated this until I reached the nominal measurement of the Allen wrench I wanted to use, and then ground the end off perfectly square and smooth. I used these "broaches" for my first trials, but found that there were two things less than perfect with these: They were brittle and thus could be easily broken off in the workpiece, and they were so hard that most methods of holding them would slip instead of digging into the broach for a good grip.

While drilling out the end of some hex keys to use as "keys" for child-proof gun safeties, I found that I couldn't drill the good ones without using a carbide drill bit. Wow, ready-made hex broaches! Cutting off about an inch of the end of a very good hex key with a Dremel Moto-tool and an abrasive cutoff disk, I flattened the end and found that it was an even better broach for my purposes.

I may have chosen a rather poor material to demonstrate in this article, but I know that by using the stainless-steel stock, I have shown that

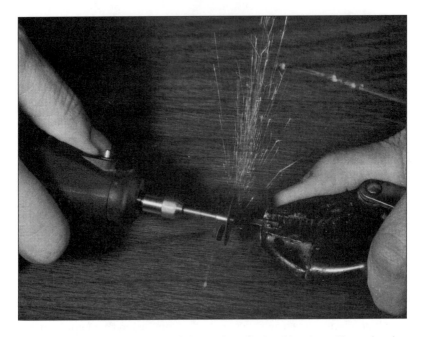

***Above:*** *A hex broach can be made by cutting off a hard hex key with an abrasive cut-off wheel in a Dremel Moto-tool.*

it can work in any metal you choose, since stainless is harder to machine well than any carbon-steel alloy. The alloy I used is the common 304 stainless, which is somewhat gummy and machines like copper—that is, it smears more readily than it cuts. This might sound like just the ticket for broaching, but it really isn't. The finish of the socket's walls are much smoother and professional-looking when a good carbon steel alloy is used. I find that I use oil-hardening drill rod bought from Brownells more than any other metal in my shop. I wouldn't have air-hardened stock in my shop for any project, as I have accidentally work-hardened it and have had to do projects over more than once in the past. I have neither the equipment nor, apparently, the know-how to truly anneal air-hardening drill rod.

The first step is to think through the project to determine what will be needed on the finished product. If the finished part is to have knurling, then the knurling must be done while the workpiece is still rigid enough to withstand the side-force caused by most knurling tools. (I have never tried one of the stressless units, but I will very soon). The workpiece must be able to be held very securely by the chuck, and the piece must be situated so that the socket end can be drilled and the broach forced into the drilled hole.

I chose to simulate the most commonly needed item with an added complication; a shoulder bolt with a hex socket head that is knurled. The first step was to chuck the stainless stock in the lathe, although it can be done with a drill press and vise. Following the drilling operation, the "broach" can be inserted with a standard "high-speed press." (I like to refer to my hammers as high-speed presses, because you can get sympathy when you tell someone that your finger is bandaged due to a high-speed press accident. Hitting your finger with a hammer, on the other hand, is just plain silly.)

After choosing the proper drill-rod diameter, or cutting it down to the approximate diameter you need, knurl it about the width you need. Remember, knurling increases the diameter as much as it impresses into the material, so don't work yourself into a position where the finished product must fit into a certain hole and won't. I usually cut a small groove into the knurling so that it looks fancier, but that's just an ego thing. While the stock is still thick, drill a hole in the end nearest the tailstock. This hole should be just the diameter of the minor diameter of the hex wrench you are planning to use on the finished product. I measure the distance from flat-to-flat with either dial calipers or digital calipers. (The minor diameter is the shortest distance across a hexagon).

After chucking the workpiece so that it is centered, I center-drill the

**Left:** *Knurling on the head of a shoulder bolt illustrates how almost any kind of hex-socket fastener can easily be made to look professional.*

*Right:* This photo shows turning a start to the shaft of the screw and starting the center drill in the location of the hex socket.

end of the workpiece to make sure that the drill to be used doesn't stray from the center of the rod. Unless you are fortunate enough to have a complete set of spotting drills, a center drill is needed. I drill with these until the 82-degree portion cuts a diameter wider than the web of the drill size I am about to use. Anything smaller than the diameter of the drill is acceptable. Be sure to use the proper cutting oil for the type of metal used.

Drilling the hole into the head end of the screw, I drill about one flat-to-flat distance in depth or more. Be careful not to drill too deep, as you will destroy all of the strength of the bolt or screw. I think that the depth of the full-diameter portion of the drill bit should be such that it leaves about one radius of material below the socket. I like to drill with sulfurated oil, but I am allergic to sulfa drugs and, evidently, to the fumes

*Left:* Drill a pilot hole for the hex socket the diameter of the flat-to-flat measurement on the hex key to be used.

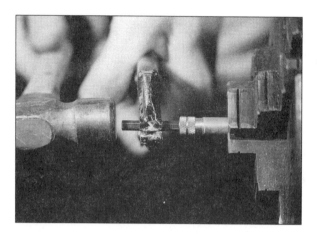

**Left:** Drive the broach into the pilot hole.

from sulfurated oils. Therefore, I use one of the tapping/cutting "wonder oils" that I get as free samples from machine-shop supply houses or at engineering trade shows.

At this point, I can decide to either leave the workpiece in the lathe, or to cut the shank diameter, re-clamp it into the chuck by the smaller diameter and allow the head to butt up against the chuck jaws for longitudinal constraint. This time, I left the workpiece in the chuck and depended upon its tightness to hold the piece. On larger hexes, this might not be a choice.

Countersink or chamfer the edges of the hole after the broaching—not before—even though chamfering would seem like a good idea to help start the broach into the hole. Doing so makes the broach more likely to expand the head of the screw instead of broaching it smoothly. If your tailstock holds a good center without being clamped to the

**Right:** After cutting the hex socket, hammer against the Vise-grip pliers to remove the broach from the finished socket.

**Left:** *Cut off the semi-finished shoulder screw on the lathe using a parting tool.*

ways, a good method of getting the broach's square end started is to grip the broach tightly with a tailstock chuck, and slide the broach into the hole with some force. If the tailstock clamps well enough to keep from sliding back, the feed screw of the tailstock can force the broach into the hole. On my smaller lathe, I always have to hold the broach into the starting marks with a pair of Vise-grip pliers and strike it repeatedly with a medium-weight ball-peen hammer.

One of the poor points of the ultra-hardened tooling-pin broaches I made is that they were brittle and couldn't be straightened out during the early part of the broaching. It may become necessary to slightly tap the hex-wrench broach to one side or the other to get it back into alignment with the axis of the screw. I have found that one that is slightly off the axis isn't really any big deal, but for those who are less tolerant than I, slight side force in the early going will correct the broach's path,

**Right:** *You can guide the threading die onto the shaft of the screw by using the tailstock's chuck face to keep the die aligned perpendicular to the axis of the screw.*

*Right: Here, the finished shoulder screw is shown with a hex key inserted into its socket. The method gives an unbelievably good fit with the wrench.*

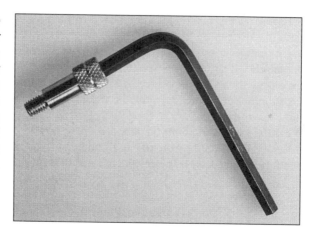

and it will stay aligned when going deeper. The harder tooling pin broaches broke off at the root of the hex when even a small side force was tried; therefore, I looked for another tool that was easier to make and more forgiving.

If you are lucky enough to have a hydraulic shop press, then the pressing of the broach into the hole can be easily controlled with a guiding fixture which prevents the broach from getting out of kilter. I suggest that you could make the same type of guide for a repeated job that would work in a bench vise.

It will be pretty evident when the broach strikes the bottom of the hole. When this is reached, the next chore is to get the broach out of the blind hole. This is another place where the more brittle tooling-pin broach tended to break. I have found no easier method than to clamp a set of Vise-grip pliers to the broach and to tap the pliers with the ball-peen hammer. Repeated, soft taps will slip it out without damaging the hex socket or the pliers. You will now be surprised at how well the standard hex wrench will fit into the new hex socket.

The last cutting job on the socket will be to countersink the opening of the socket with a standard countersink tool. This helps to guide the wrench into the socket, and makes the socket look more professional. The broached end of the head can be Scotchbrite smoothed and buffed on a cloth polishing wheel to get the head looking sharp.

Finally, the device should have the threads cut into it—if threading is required. I usually use a threading die if the threads are standard, but it may be necessary to chuck the workpiece up again in the lathe to single-point cut the threads. If you have knurled the head, I would suggest that a strip of brass shimstock be wrapped around the knurling to prevent damage from the jaws.

I also use the tailstock chuck's face to help align the threading die with the shaft of the screw. As I turn the die handle, I advance the tailstock quill to keep the chuck in full contact with the rear of the die or die handle. If the threads are to be all the way up to the shoulder, as they are with a shoulder screw, then I would either cut a relief next to the shoulder or I would turn the die around backwards to cut the threads right up to the shoulder.

A final hint: Run some blackboard chalk on the threads for the last pass with the threading die to clean and burnish the threads, and I think you'll be amazed with the results of your first hex socket job. ★

# 12.

# Caustic Bluing Alternatives

*Even if disposing of bluing salts costs too much,
you can stay in the gun-refinishing
business with these items.*

By Chick Blood

Until the 1940s, knowing how to blue guns was a well-kept secret held by a few masters of the craft. It was a long, labor intensive process that required hours of rubbing, scrubbing, and polishing followed by many days of controlled rusting and burnishing. It often involved witches' brews, the formulas for which were known only to the artisans who created them. One of the simpler methods called for the use of nitric acid. Full strength.

The late Bob Brownell changed all that. When he introduced Oxynate No. 7 bluing salts 47 years ago, he made it possible for just about anybody to perform their own hot-bluing jobs. But in spite of the simplicity Brownell brought to the process, if you live in or near a high-density population area, you may not be able to provide complete rebluing services. For one thing, bluing salts are caustic. Though a solution of them can be renewed to last for months unless it becomes contaminated, disposing of salts and other bluing chemicals can be costly. The brick wall I ran into when considering whether or not to handle my own bluing serves as a good example.

I planned to install standard, 4½-gallon tanks: one of black iron for the bluing solution and three of stainless steel. The stainless cleaning tank should be dumped daily. I soon found out that local ordinances would not allow me to pour it down the municipal drain or construct a dry well into which it could be poured. A combination of local, state, and federal regulations absolutely prohibited dumping of caustic bluing salt solutions at any time.

Therefore, salt and cleaning solutions both had to be professionally

**Left:** Bob Brownell's Oxynate No. 7 broke the cloak of secrecy about gun bluing 47 years ago. However, it's caustic, and that can lead to expensive disposal costs.

disposed of by contract with an authorized, approved and otherwise official handler of toxic waste. The cost of that contract? Sixty dollars for each 5-gallon container and no, I couldn't supply my own. My math marched depressingly onward. Original investment in major equipment not on hand: $2,935. Assorted chemicals: $125. One month's worth of 5-gallon containers: $1,200. Disposal of same once a month: $150 plus tax. Plus propane to heat the solutions. Plus odds and ends like a small-parts basket, plumbing, and bluing accessories.

Costs and regulations are going to vary according to where you live, so check out local laws before letting me discourage you from adding gun bluing to your list of services. Even if you find the expense and complications extreme, as I did, you're still not totally out of the gun refinishing business. You can always provide touch-up service for scrapes and scratches with cold blue solutions. Or you can work out a deal with a good, full-time, commercial operation offering discounts to gunsmiths.

## Alternative One

One option is Dicropan IM, a noncaustic "hot bluing" fluid. The only thing that could prevent you from using this process is if your local authorities are as paranoid as mine about pouring cleaning solution into their sewer. It can be done with a two-tank set up, so it makes a nice fit for a small shop or even an individual who wants to blue a gun every so often. One tank is of fiberglass, for water-displacing oil. The other tank, either stainless steel or black iron, is used for both the cleaning solution and to hold boiling water. You start the process by degreasing a couple of steel-wool pads in 1,1,1 trichlorethane and allowing them to dry completely.

While they're drying, mix up a fresh batch of Dicro-Pan 909 cleaning solution at the rate of 5 ounces of 909 to a gallon of clean water. You'll need enough to completely cover the piece you're cleaning. Heat up the solution to exactly 180 degrees, stirring it frequently, and stabilize it at that temperature. Suspend the piece in the hot solution and keep it submerged for 2 to 15 minutes, depending on the crud to be removed. Once it's out of the tank, rinse the piece thoroughly under a faucet or with a garden hose, shake off the excess water and lay it on some paper towels to dry.

Being careful not to burn yourself, empty the cleaning solution into a heat-proof container for later disposal and flush out the tank with running water. Next, fill the tank with fresh water to a minimum depth of 4 inches and start bringing it to a rolling boil. When it has reached that point, maintain the boil while you suspend the piece in the water for 5 minutes, remove it from the tank and allow it to air dry.

Using those degreased steel-wool pads I mentioned earlier, vigorously rub the surface of the metal to remove any rust that may have formed. Don't worry about any slight discoloration you may spot in the metal itself; they clear up in the next step and generally have no effect on the final color. The next step has its beginning back while you were waiting for the cleaning solution to do its job. You first pour some Dicro-pan IM into a deep-sided ceramic dish or polyethylene container. You then make two swabs by cutting two, 4-inch lengths from the leg of a pair of panty hose. You tie one end of each closed, stuff each "bag" with a two handfuls of cotton balls and tie a knot in the other end. The result should be about twice the size of a golf ball.

Soak one of these oversized duffer's delights liberally in the Dicro-pan and apply it to the entire metal surface. Don't worry about runs or streaks. Slosh on as much as you can for about a minute, making sure you don't miss any part of the surface, then resuspend the piece in the boiling water. When you take it out 5 minutes later, you'll think the worst has happened. It will be covered with muddy brown crud. It will have splotches and other discoloration. Don't worry, it's supposed to, but if you don't handle the horror before you exactly as I am about to describe, you will end up starting all over again.

Once the piece is dry, everything you touch it with must be dry. Bone dry. Your gloves. Steel wool. Whatever. If any part of that brown mud gets wet now, it will leave a stain only repolishing can remove. Hold the part with a wooden plug or some other solid holding method while you vigorously rub off the crud and misery with the same steel wool pad you used previously. Rub hard enough and long enough to remove any blemishes and discoloration and turn the pad frequently to give yourself a fresh working surface.

Using the second swab you prepared, apply the second coat of Dicropan IM as liberally as you did before, for as long as you did before, then place the piece back into the boiling water. Five minutes later, take it out, let it air dry and use your second degreased, dry steel wool pad to rub it down hard. You keep applying the Dicropan, boiling the piece for five minutes, letting it dry and rubbing it with the same steel wool until you get the uniform, blue color you're after. This usually means five or six coats, but you can deepen the blue with additional coats.

After that color has been reached, give the piece a final inspection under an ordinary light bulb. Any minor blemishes you see will likely disappear after an overnight stay in the water-displacing oil tank. Larger blemishes should be attacked with a freshly degreased and dried steel wool pad. If these blemishes persist, don't try and touch them up. Applying another coat of Dicropan, boiling it and rubbing it down is the advised way to get these color variations to blend in. Once they are, suspend the piece in water-displacing oil and leave it there for the night. This final soaking not only "cures" the bluing job, it actually replaces every water molecule with a molecule of oil for the finest rust protection available.

## Alternative Two

The second option is baking lacquer, a coating the British used during World War II that speeded up the production of combat weapons and provided excellent protection in the field. You don't need anything but a household oven, paint booth and spray gun or air brush to use it, and if you don't have a spray gun or air brush, it's available in aerosol cans. Brownells offers it in clear, gloss black and flat black. You can use the clear to get a close match with the gray finish used by some gun manufacturers on their higher grade shotgun and rifle receivers. The gloss or matte black is ideal for hard to blue items like cast iron or aluminum receivers, forend irons, Winchester post-'64 receivers, non-ferrous metal trigger groups and stainless steel parts. The matte black also comes in very handy for transforming the shiny metal of a frequently used hunting rifle or shotgun to a dull finish that won't spook game.

The first thing to do before using a baking lacquer is to make sure the barrel, or barreled action, will fit in your oven. Might not be a bad idea to also make sure it's OK with your significant other for you to use the oven. The next thing to do is rig up some sort of spray booth. You can put one together out of ³/₈-inch plywood or simply locate a good sized cardboard box. Cut a hole in the top or back that fits the hose of a shop vacuum to suck out any overspray. Whether you end up with wood or cardboard, figure out a way to suspend the piece you're going to be spraying. Wire from coathangers works well and is easy to work with. I bend a couple of lengths with an "L" at each end, work one end down of each through a small hole in the top of the "booth" and suspend the barrel by its muzzle and breech. If I'm doing a barreled action for a rifle, I still suspend the piece by its muzzle and breech after removing the bolt. If it's a shotgun receiver, I hang it by the ejection port. Any pins or screws removed from a receiver that will show

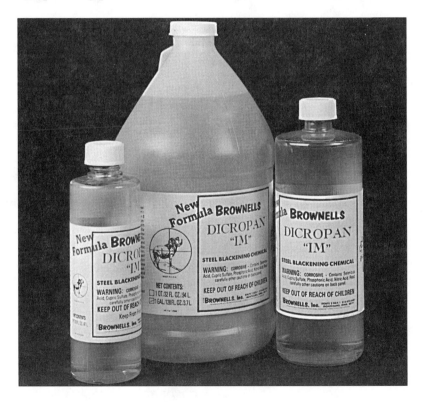

*Above:* Dicropan IM provides a noncaustic "hot bluing" technique that only requires a single tank, which makes it a good option for the small shop or the individual wanting to do an occasional bluing job.

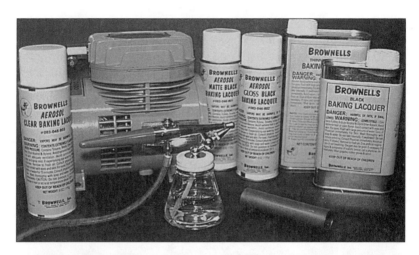

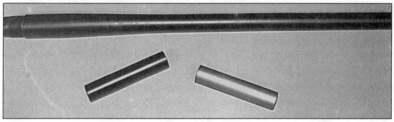

*Above: Brownells baking lacquers are coatings, not a finish. They totally elimi-nate disposal problems and can be applied with spraying equipment or from aerosol cans. The barrel pieces show the flat-black coating (top), gloss-black coating (bottom left), and clear coat. All three can be cured in a kitchen oven.*

externally on reassembly must be sprayed to match the new finish.

Prepping a barrel, barreled action, or receiver for baking lacquer ap-plication is far simpler than prepping one for bluing. Whatever you're working on should be cleaned with 1,1,1 Trichlorethane to remove any dirt, oil, silicones, or grease. This is followed by brushing with a 0.005 or 0.006 wire wheel turning at about 1750 rpm with all brushing done parallel to the bore line: lengthwise—not across the barrel.

With clear lacquer, you don't have to polish the brushed surface brighter than 500 grit polishing compound will make it. For black lac-quer, don't go above 400 grit. If you make the surface to be coated too slick, poor adhesion may result. To further protect yourself from that possibility, you may elect to have the piece finely bead blasted at low pressure after polishing. Next, soak the piece in 1,1,1 Trichlorethane for half an hour to remove any grit from the polishing and allow it to

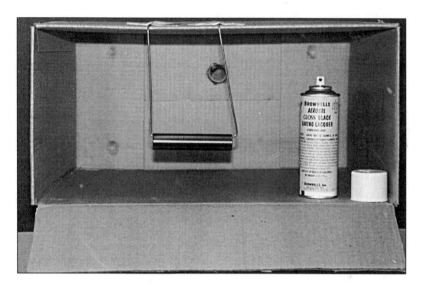

**Above:** *The low-tech professional spray booth (above) was made from a card-board box. The hose showing in the rear is a shop vacuum installed to remove overspray. The object that looks like a toilet-tissue holder was made from clothes-hanger to support segments during spraying.*

air-dry completely. Do not use compressed air to dry it unless the air has been passed through a filter. When you handle the part, use clean cotton polishing gloves.

Unless you're using the pre-mixed, aerosol spray version of this product, the proper proportion for your spray gun or air brush ought to be four parts lacquer to one part thinner. You may have to tinker a little bit to get the right mix for your equipment. With any equipment, though, it's important that it's delivering clean, dry air to prevent contamination of the lacquer. A filter/moisture trap in the air system assures that it will.

You apply the lacquer in thin, even passes until all bare areas are covered, then leave it to dry for 2 hours. About 15 minutes before the 2 hours is up, preheat your oven to 325 degrees, then place the coated piece in it to cure for 20 minutes. That's it. There are no disposal problems and the finish is every bit as tough as the coated finishes you'll find on factory guns. ★

# Section Two

# Techniques

# 13.

# Setting Up A Work Area For Gunsmithing

*You'll find cleaning and basic maintenance easier to manage if you have everything in a designated spot. Here are some ideas.*

*By Dennis A. Wood*

Cleaning before storage is one of the most important things you can do to prevent damage to your costly firearms. You only have to put an uncleaned gun used during wet, snowy or rainy conditions away for the season one time to learn a costly lesson, especially if it's stored in a carrying case. Next fall, when you pull that firearm out for an anticipated hunt, it will no doubt greet you with a new, furry red skin. A catastrophe like that can be averted with just a little attention to the firearms before they go into storage.

A work bench dedicated just to maintenance of your firearms need not take up a lot of room and, if arranged according to your needs, can remove some of the drudgery of firearms cleaning. The convenience of having an area that contains all your tools makes working on your firearms much more pleasant.

A good start for most is a work bench measuring 4 to 6 feet in length, about 2 feet front to back, and 34 inches high anchored to the wall and floor. Sturdiness and rigidity of construction is an absolute plus. You don't need to be chasing the bench around the room and a wobbly bench is, at best, frustrating to deal with. Consider acquiring some pre-assembled base cabinets that are available at most of the larger lumber yards. These cabinets can be found in pine or birch-faced plywood and are usually priced reasonably. Most of these base cabinets can be purchased with a top drawer and a door that opens to expose a shelved storage area for cleaning supplies. Anchored to the floor and wall, they become quite solid. A $3/4$-to-1 inch top made of plywood and screwed in place makes a nice, flat working surface.

***Above:*** *A set of Magna-tip bits will fit almost any gun-screw slot that exists.*

Sealing the top with several coats of varnish will prevent gun crud from permeating the raw plywood top.

Once your bench has been secured, and any movement eliminated, the next item of importance to consider is a sturdy vise. Unfortunately, we were born with only two hands even though a third would be greatly appreciated when disassembling firearms for cleaning or whatever. This is where the vise comes in handy. It doesn't have to be expensive, but it should be sturdy. A cast-iron vise, with jaws at least 4 inches wide, that has a swiveling base will not set you back much dollar-wise. Some of the imported vises coming into this country are priced so low that you sometimes wonder if they don't push the people who make them out the tenth floor window on Friday rather than pay them.

When mounted to a sturdy bench with bolts through the vise base and bench you'll have a solid setup. Most vises normally come with serrated jaw faces. As is, such jaw faces are not very kind to the finishes we need to maintain on firearms. A set of false jaws for your vise can be fashioned out of almost any hardwood. With some $1/4$-inch thick leather glued to the inside faces of these false jaws, you'll protect the finish on any gun. If you feel you'd like to get more elaborate, Brownells sells material for false jaws specifically formulated for dealing with either metal or wood surfaces.

If you are like me, you've had to accompany the wife at least once to shop for carpeting. No doubt you've also had to suffer through the endless viewing of samples that the salesperson is all too willing to show you. These carpet samples, usually sized around 18 x 24 inches, make great bench mats. If you're purchasing carpet, work out a deal with the salesperson to get a half dozen or so of these sample pads thrown in. Otherwise, they can be found from 50 cents to a dollar anywhere carpet is sold. These pads are great for disassembly of handguns, as parts usually stay on them and when they get overly dirty can be tossed away. I prefer short nap samples, as the deep pile variety has a tendency to allow small pins and screws a place to hide.

The best investment you will ever make as far as firearms maintenance is concerned is a set of good hollow ground screwdriver bits. The importance of a properly fitting screwdriver blade cannot be overstated. We've all seen screw slots butchered by some gun owner using a tapered blade screwdriver. Battered screw slots can make an otherwise nice firearm look atrocious. Magna-tip hollow ground screwdriver bits are sold in sets or individually at affordable cost so there is no excuse to not use them.

Every width and thickness ever contrived for screw slots has a representative screwdriver bit available for it. If a bit is broken, a replacement can be found for about $2.

Maintaining firearms so that they remain in reliable condition often means they will need to be taken down in either subassemblies or completely for a thorough cleaning. Another set of tools that will prove invaluable will be a good set of drift pin punches. Starrett and General are two brands that come to mind as they are readily available in sets or individually. Diameters of these punches run from 0.060 inch on up.

A 2-ounce ballpeen hammer will provide enough power for most pin drifting and a pair of safety glasses should always accompany the use of drifting punches. A bench block, either steel or nylon, is also a handy item. These round blocks, which resemble a cup, have several different sizes of holes in them and usually a v-groove. Their job is to support the off side of the firearm over the appropriate hole in the block and then drift out the pin. The hollowed out underside of the bench block acts as a captivating chamber for the removed pin.

For drifting front or rear sights, using a brass drift will often be recommended. I'm not a fan of the use of brass punches on blued surfaces, because brass drifts almost always leave behind a residual yellow smear that isn't easy to remove. I purchased a solid copper rod, 6 feet in length and 3/8-inch diameter, well over 10 years ago. I've cut about six 4-inch lengths off it to use for drifting front and rear sights. Copper is softer than brass but I think it makes a better drift. The smear that's left behind can be wiped off a blued surface much easier.

*Above:* A vise doesn't have to be expensive, but it should be sturdy. Most come with serrated jaws. To protect the gun's finish, you can make a set of false jaws from almost any hardwood and glue leather pieces to them.

All this equipment is not going to do you much good without sufficient lighting to get the cleaning job done properly and thoroughly. Find a good lamp that has a bent arm and swiveling head and can handle a 100-watt bulb. You can point this type of light in almost any direction and peer into the nooks and crannies that hold gunk.

If I had to pick only two of the seemingly infinite variety of gun solvents available, Shooter's Choice and Break-Free CLP would be the ones that would have a spot reserved on my bench. There are a lot of brands out there to choose from, and I try just about every new one in search of the ultimate solution. Most people don't. These brands have served me well, so I don't think you'd go wrong with them.

The aforementioned equipment should set you up with a convenient area to help in the maintenance of your firearms.

A dedicated, organized area, containing all the tools and supplies you need to get the job done somewhat guarantees that the job will get done. If you have to search around gathering up all the things necessary to clean your firearms until the next season arrives, the job can all too often get neglected.

A last suggestion would be to make sure you leave a spot on the end of your bench for your *American Gunsmith* books and magazine binders. ★

# 14.

# Using The Versatile Rotary Tool

*If you don't already own one of these handy little tools, you're doing a lot of things the hard way. If you do, here's how to get the most out of it.*

T
here is seemingly no end to the timesaving devices available for the gunsmith. Specialty tools and fixtures abound for assisting in the reassembly of parts, for example, the fitting and altering of sights, and just about any other task you might want to take on. Anytime elbow action can be replaced with a reasonably priced tool, my interest is piqued. But the one power tool I could not do without is my Dremel rotary tool.

*by Dennis A. Wood*

The model #332 Moto-Flex rotary tool I use has a flexible shaft going from the motor to the handpiece, making it easy to manipulate in tight places. The addition of a variable-speed power control gives a wider selection of revolutions per minute for the various tools that happen to be chucked in the collet at the time of use. This gives the tool more versatility when dealing with the different materials involved when working on firearms.

The rotary tool's handpiece contains the interchangeable collets that hold the shafts of the various tools needed to get through the job at hand. For the most part, a $^1/_8$-inch collet is used, but the occasional $^3/_{32}$-inch shaft on other manufacturers' accessories will require the use of this size collet.

Chucking the proper tool in the collet—and donning protective eyewear, of course—makes the tool ready for a variety of tasks. Many of those tools, as well as the tasks they're used for, are detailed below:

## Grinding Stones
For metal removal, miniature grinding wheels mounted on a $^1/_8$-inch

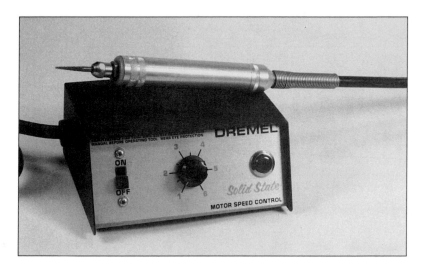

**Above:** *The flexible-shaft rotary tool is even more versatile with a variable-speed power control.*

shaft are available in shapes such as cone, cylinder, ball, and disk. The various shapes come in handy for getting into just about any area imaginable, like the corners around a newly welded bolt handle to remove excess weld metal. And reshaping a standard military trigger guard with these shafted stones can give it a more appealing custom look in much less time than filing. Another example: A Mauser or Springfield magazine follower can receive a ground bevel on the rear to allow complete bolt closure after the magazine has been emptied, eliminating the need to push the follower down with a finger.

Bolt shrouds that have become pitted over the years from rust can get a smooth new surface with a stone in a rotary tool. If you have a metal lathe, you know how difficult it can be grinding a radius into a tool bit for barrel crowning. By using a shafted grinding stone dressed to the proper diameter, grinding a tool bit radius becomes a much easier task. I once needed to make a top lever for an old double-barrel shotgun. The whole thing was rough shaped out of a piece of steel with shafted grinding stones and a rotary tool, and then finished with files. Yes, it was somewhat time consuming, but it took less time than if I had done the whole job with files.

## Abrasive Cutoff Wheels

One-inch-diameter and 1¹/₄-inch-diameter abrasive cutoff wheels probably don't get the call to duty very often, but, when they're needed, they're nice to have close at hand. These wheels will cut anything that a hacksaw blade will cut—and quite a few materials that the saw teeth will just skid across. A military bolt handle can be cut off in short order with one of these wheels, for example. And large-diameter springs can be easily trimmed to length with these abrasive wheels—even those that can't be cut with a wire nipper.

The only caution to be aware of when using these little cutoff wheels is to avoid excessive side pressure that could cause the wheel to break.

## Polishing

This is one of the more frequent tasks required of my rotary tool. Hard felt points and wheels charged with different grades of polishing compound can get into areas not easily accessible by other means. In and around trigger guards, cylinder flutes, and feed ramps are just some of the areas that come to mind that will require the occasional pre-bluing polish during restoration work.

There are many different styles and shapes of grit-impregnated rubber wheels and points. These are quite handy for rust removal and the smoothing of tool marks left behind from manufacturing. The internal surface of a revolver side plate will often benefit from smoothing the milling marks left behind, especially where they interact with the moving hammer and trigger parts. Any tight area that requires a smoother surface can usually be reached with the proper size and shape tool.

## Wire Wheels and Brushes

Anyone who has been doing gun repair for any length of time has probably cleaned more firearms than he can remember. The ones you do remember are those that were so gunked up you wondered how in the world they were ever able to function at all—or perhaps they were

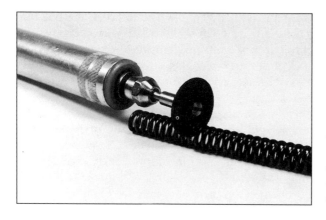

**Left:** A cutoff wheel will cut heavier springs even when a nipper won't.

brought to you because they didn't function. Small wire wheels and end brushes, when run in a rotary tool, will greatly reduce the time it takes to remove accumulations of light rust and crud.

The three shapes used most often are the end-style brush, the cup style, and the round wire wheel. These little brushes can also be used to remove the old blued surface from metal surfaces, and as an alternative to bead blasting for getting the rust out of small surface pits.

## Burr Bits

Small rotary cutters are available in cylindrical, ball, oval, and tapered-end shapes. Burr bits can be obtained in high-speed steel, carbide, and coated carbide. Also available are burrs that are impregnated with diamond particles; these will handle the shaping of everything from aluminum alloy to hardened steels. The carbide cutters will do everything that the high-speed steel cutters will do and more, and they'll last a lot longer.

A $^3/_{16}$-inch ball burr bit will remove wood or fiberglass quickly when preparing a stock for a glass bedding job. The tiny $^1/_{32}$-inch ball burr will re-cut a badly battered screw slot so that a screwdriver can be used to remove the screw for repair or replacement. The tapered-end carbide burrs will get you through blending an add-on flared magazine chute with the edges of the magazine well, and do it much more quickly than a file will. A beavertail grip safety can also be blended into the rear of the frame in a lot less time.

One thing to be aware of with the use of these burr-type cutters is the tiny slivers created with metal removal. These little metal slivers have a tendency to embed themselves in your fingers; wearing gloves is a good idea.

Have you ever broken a tap when you were just about three-quar-

**Left:** Polishing the flutes of a revolver cylinder goes much quicker with a rotary tool.

ters of the way through the hole? The $^1/_{32}$-inch carbide or diamond ball burr bit will eat up a broken carbon tap stuck in a hole so that the remaining pieces can be removed. The diamond impregnated variety will take care of the high-speed steel taps if the tool is run slowly while grinding out the center of the tap, all the while trying not to hit the sides of the threaded hole. With caution, it can be done.

## Sanding Drums

A small sanding drum is handy to have for sanding radiused areas. The little rubber drums hold $^1/_2$-inch diameter sanding sleeves in course and fine grits. The sleeve is slipped onto the sanding drum and then a screw is tightened on the front of the drum, expanding the sleeve, to keep it in place.

## Conclusion

There are several brands and styles of rotary-type power tools available to the gunsmith. The brands that come to mind are those offered by Dremel, Foredom, and the imported tools from Enco. A variable-speed selection is a definite advantage for doing any work on firearms. Those tools that use steel rather than nylon bearings will hold up longer and help the collet hold shafts without developing wobble over time.

Consider buying a small-diameter handpiece, since these are more comfortable to hold and will help in getting into tight areas such as receivers and side rails. Once you discover the usefulness of the rotary tool, it will be as hard to get away from you as a bedroom slipper from a puppy. ★

# 15.

# Stock Carving: Patterns, Design Application

*Special techniques and tricks allow you to execute carvings on many different gunstock areas, the most important of which is the buttstock.*

*By Philip Eck*

The gunstock carver may place designs on many different areas of the gunstock, including the forearm tip, forearm grip, side receiver area, pistol grip, buttstock, pistol grip cap, and buttplate. However, each area requires special techniques to execute the designs properly, and of these areas, the buttstock generally receives the most designs. Here are a few hints you need to know to properly place carvings on buttstock wood.

## Buttstock Techniques

The buttstock is the part of the gunstock most often carved. It is usually carved on the off side, which is the side that faces away from the shooter when the gun is held in firing position.

Depending on how elaborate a client wishes the stock to be, it can also be carved on the cheekpiece side. When carving on the cheekpiece side it is best to follow the basic guidelines set forth in the section covering cheekpiece patterns.

To determine the size of the area that can be carved, and to maintain the exact positioning of the design once it has been determined, you need to be able to tape the design pattern sheet to the stock, remove it, and place it back in precisely the same position. For this purpose you will need to use locator tapes, such as pieces of 1-inch-wide masking tape.

On a straight stock (Figure A) place a 1-inch to 2-inch piece of tape lengthwise across the top of the stock with at least half its width on wood and the remainder overlapping the buttplate or recoil pad. Ap-

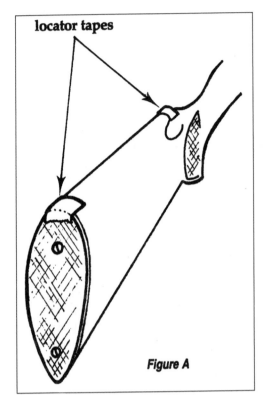

locator tapes

**Figure A**

*Figure A, left:* On a straight stock place a 1-inch to 2-inch piece of tape lengthwise across the top of the stock with at least half its width on wood and the remainder overlapping the buttplate or recoil pad. Approximately half the length of the tape should be on each side of the stock. Place a second piece of tape in a similar manner across the top of the stock at the drop of the comb just above the grip. These are the top-of-stock forward and rear locator tapes.

proximately half the length of the tape should be on each side of the stock. Place a second piece of tape in a similar manner across the top of the stock at the drop of the comb just above the grip. These are the top-of-stock forward and rear locator tapes.

Now, using a pad as protection against damage, lay the stock on its cheekpiece side with the off side facing up. Place a full sheet of tracing paper onto the stock, carefully aligning one of the short edges of the paper with the inside edge of the buttplate or recoil pad. Keep the approximate center of the paper running lengthwise at the center of the side area of the buttstock from front to rear. This doesn't need to be exact; there's ample paper to compensate for any deviation. What's important is that the paper follows the contour of the inside edge of the buttplate where it meets the wood of the buttstock and that a nearly equal amount of paper running along that edge falls on each side of the buttstock. Be sure the positioning of the paper from front to rear enables the outline marking of the ball of thumb recess and rear border line of the checkered grip panel, which is the maximum forward area of a buttstock carving. Use a small piece of masking tape to secure the paper at each end at the center of the stock's side area. The paper should be lying flat against the wood and pulled reasonably taut between the securing tapes but not so taut as to cause a pull line or ripple. The rear securing tape should overlap no more than $^1/_4$ inch onto the paper.

Once the paper is securely attached at each end, fold the upper half across the top of the stock, then bring it downward to lie flat on the opposite side (Figure B). Check to make sure the forward locator tape at the top of the stock is only half covered by the paper. You may have to move this tape or trim the paper to allow half coverage. Then pull the paper lightly taut, and place a securing tape at the center of the paper along its edge on the cheekrest side. Working outward from this piece of tape, space additional securing tapes in spots along the entire edge. Fold the bottom half of the paper around the underside of the stock, and secure this edge in the same manner.

When you are certain the paper is in the proper position with no

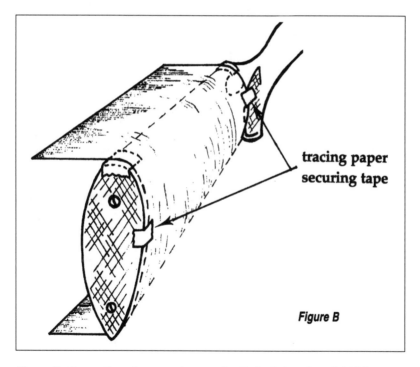

tracing paper

securing tape

*Figure B*

*Figure B, above:* Once the paper is securely attached at each end, fold the upper half across the top of the stock, then bring it downward to lie flat on the opposite side. Check to make sure the forward locator tape at the top of the stock is only half covered by the paper. You may have to move this tape or trim the paper to allow half coverage.

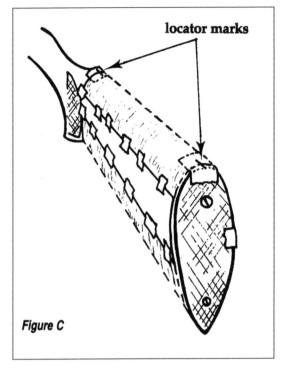

locator marks

**Figure C**

**Figure C, left:** *Now turn the stock upright and look straight down at the locator tapes. Determine the center point of thickness of the stock, and draw a pencil mark running off the paper from the center onto each of the tapes. These marks will enable you to place the pattern back onto the stock in this exact position after you have traced the design.*

pulls or ripples, place additional securing tapes on the buttplate and checkered area edges on the off side above and below the tapes at the center. Make certain there are no ripples, folds, or creases anywhere in the paper on the side where the design will go.

Now turn the stock upright and look straight down at the locator tapes. Determine the center point of thickness of the stock, and draw a pencil mark running off the paper from the center onto each of the tapes (Figure C). These marks should be about ¹/₂ inch in length, with about ¹/₄ inch each on the paper and the tape. These marks will enable you to place the pattern back onto the stock in this exact position after you have traced the design. Recheck the pencil centerline marks to make certain they are at center of the thickness of the stock. Make any needed correction, then darken the locator marks on both paper and tape with a dark, fine-point felt-tip pen. Next, using the side of the lead of a pencil, draw a full-length line connecting the inked locator marks. Do not draw this line with the point of the pencil; doing so is likely to cause an indentation in the finish of the stock. Keep the line as near straight as possible, but don't be overly concerned with minor irregularities. Make a similar full-length mark on the paper down the center of the bottom portion of the buttstock. Again using the side of the lead, lightly draw a line following the contour of the inner edge of the butt-plate but about $^3/_8$ inch in on the paper. At both buttplate and grip ends, place a short, lightly drawn horizontal pencil mark 1 inch inward toward the center of the side of the stock from the top and bottom centerline-of-stock marks. At the grip end, draw a line showing the location of the upper edge of the ball-of-thumb recess and rear borderline of the checkering. When connected (Figure D), these marks (Figure E) will show the overall area available for carving. Do not connect the marks with the longer area-defining lines while the paper is on the stock. Remove the paper from the stock, place it on a flat surface, and connect the lines with a straightedge. This line is referred to as the maximum-area-of-coverage line.

## Monte Carlo Cheekpieces

The process of establishing the carving area on a stock with a high cheekpiece at the top, known as a Monte Carlo-type stock, is similar to what I've just described, but there are differences in the placement of the rear locator tape and the positioning of the paper to allow for the shape of the stock (Figure F). Otherwise, the area marks can be clearly defined following the same procedure as with the straight stock (Figure G).

Only on rare occasions is the entire area of the off side of the buttstock ever carved. Most times the focal point of a carving is located at the area near the butt-plate end of the stock.

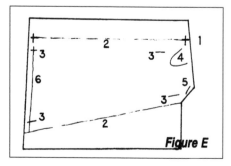

*Figure D and E, left:* At the grip end, draw a line showing the location of the upper edge of the ball-of-thumb recess and rear borderline of the checkering. When connected, these marks will show the overall area available for carving. Do not connect the marks with the longer area-defining lines while the paper is on the stock. Remove the paper from the stock, place it on a flat surface, and connect the lines with a straightedge. This line is referred to as the maximum-area-of-coverage line.

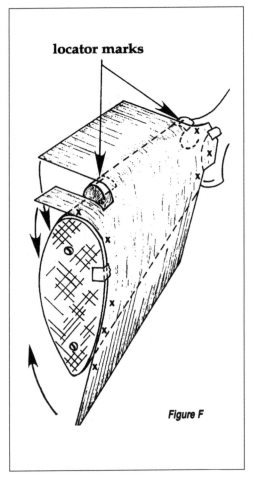

**locator marks**

Figure F

*Figure F and G, left and below:*

*On Monte Carlo-type stocks,there are differences in the placement of the rear locator tape and the positioning of the paper to allow for the shape of the stock. Otherwise, the area marks can be clearly defined following the same procedure as with the straight stock.*

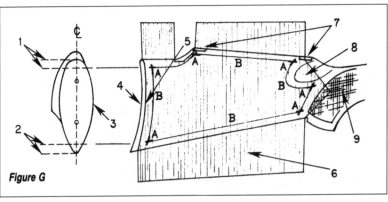

Figure G

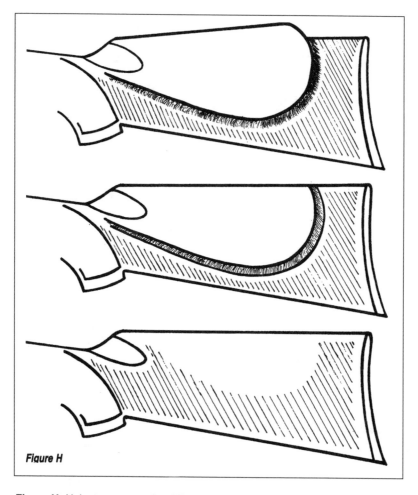

**Figure H**

**Figure H:** *Unless you are quite skilled and can execute a very shallow carving, don't carve the area where the shooter rests the cheek. Instead, confine all carving to the shaded areas shown.*

Carving on the cheekpiece side of the buttstock is not often requested, but I encourage the carving of this area. When it is carved in harmony with other carved areas, it adds a dimension that is both unusual and very appealing.

A raised cheekpiece begins at the same plane as the lower portion of the buttstock at the area of the grip. As it progresses to the rear it gradually rises until it reaches its full height at its rearmost portion. This rise is usually ³/₄ inch, but it can vary with individual stocks. Stocks vary

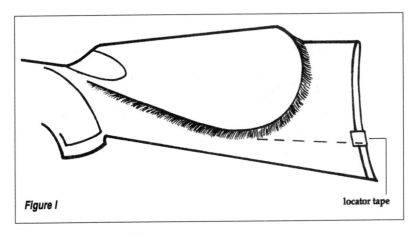

**Figure I**                                                    locator tape

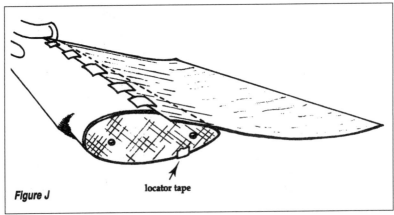

**Figure J**                          locator tape

*Figures I and J, above:* To lay out a pattern for the area below a raised cheek-piece of either straight or Monte Carlo–type stock, first place as a locator a small piece of masking tape on the buttplate, overlapping about ¹/₄ inch onto the stock in line with the bottom curve of the cheekpiece. Place the stock on a pad with the cheekpiece facing down. Tape a full sheet of tracing paper securely on the off side of the stock, lengthwise from front to rear, positioning one of the longer edges of the paper near the center of the buttstock side. Then, turn the stock over and fold the paper under the bottom of the stock to cover the area below the cheekpiece.

in design, and a raised cheekpiece will end either very near the butt-plate or as much as 2 inches from the buttplate. This rise creates a two-level configuration to the cheekpiece side of the stock with the lower portion maintaining a uniform configuration with the opposite side of the stock. As the cheek-piece rises, the area of wood from the line of the upper edge of the cheek-piece to the lower area of the buttstock becomes more pronounced. The ex-treme upper edge of the cheekpiece begins as little more than a scratch at the grip area where both the upper and lower areas are on the same plane but with the rise of the cheekpiece the area between levels increases. As stock configura-tions do vary, the connect-

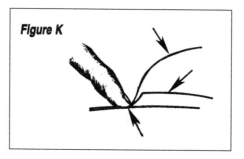

**Figure K**

**Figure K, above:** *With the tip of a fingernail, lightly press the paper flat to the stock below the raised cheekpiece, moving the finger upward from the bottom of the stock to the lowest part of the curve of the cheekpiece at the stock's flat lower surface.*

ing area of wood is sometimes cut straight from one level to the other, or it might have a slight curve downward and outward from the upper edge of the cheekpiece to the lower area. This connecting area of wood is considered part of the cheekpiece, not part of the lower portion of the buttstock. When laying out a design on the pattern sheet, mark the entire length of the line that meets the lower configuration of the buttstock. This line and the centerline-of-stock mark along the bottom of the stock predetermine the vertical limits of the carving area. You need only lay out tracing paper to suit the curve of the cheekpiece at its underside. Unless you are quite skilled and can execute a very shal-low carving, I do not recommend carving the area where the shooter rests his or her cheek, as it could very well be a source of discomfort to the shooter. If you do decide to carve on the raised portion of the cheekpiece, keep it confined to a thin portion following the contour of the cheekpiece just above its edge (Figure H). To avoid an over-worked appearance, there should be no other carving on that side of the buttstock running below the cheekpiece, except possibly at the toe of the stock. Should you carve the toe area as well, both areas must be in harmony with each other and with any carving on the pistol grip and forearm.

## Lay Out Pattern

To lay out a pattern for the area below a raised cheekpiece of either straight or Monte Carlo–type stock, first place as a locator a small piece of masking tape on the buttplate, overlapping about 1/4 inch onto the

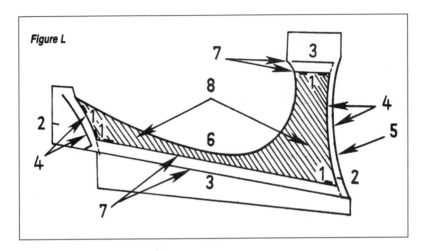

**Figure L, above:** *Mark a full-length line on the paper along the center of the buttstock underside from buttplate to grip area, then make a light ¹/₄-inch-long line on the cheekpiece side at each end of the pattern sheet at 1 inch from, and parallel with, the centerline-of-stock mark. Place two marks ³/₈ to ¹/₂ inch rearward of the border of the checkering, one at the top and one at the bottom. You will use these ¹/₄-inch lines, in conjunction with the marks at the grip and butt areas, to outline the exact area open for carving.*

stock in line with the bottom curve of the cheekpiece (Figure I). Place the stock on a pad with the cheekpiece facing down. Tape a full sheet of tracing paper securely on the off side of the stock, lengthwise from front to rear, positioning one of the longer edges of the paper near the center of the buttstock side. Then, turn the stock over and fold the paper under the bottom of the stock to cover the area below the cheekpiece (Figure J). Position the rear short edge of the paper to match the line of the buttplate or project slightly beyond the butt end of the stock, ensuring that all of the wood along the line of the buttplate is covered. With the paper extending beyond the buttplate, you can mark the inside edge of the buttplate where it meets wood. Place another mark ³/₈ to ¹/₂ inch from the buttplate; this will serve as the rear boundary line for the carving. All marks on this side of the stock pattern sheet are to be made after the paper is securely taped.

To achieve a correct fit of the paper on the cheekpiece side after you've secured it to the off side, adjust the stock so that it's lying on the off side with the paper flat, extending well beyond the bottom edge of the stock. Pull the paper upward and lay it over the cheekpiece. With the tip of a fingernail, lightly press the paper flat to the stock below the raised cheekpiece, moving the finger upward from the bottom of the stock to the lowest part of the curve of the cheekpiece at the stock's flat lower surface (Figure K). Use a felt-tip pen to place a small dot on the paper at the point of the fingernail where it meets the beginning of the rise of the cheekpiece. Repeat this procedure at $^{1}/_{2}$-inch intervals from the lowest point of the curve of the cheekpiece to its ending point near the pistol grip. At this time, do not attempt to place marks along the portion of the curve rounding upward toward the top of the stock nearest the butt end.

After you have made the marks on the grip area, turn the stock to lie on the cheekpiece side, allowing the paper to be straightened. Then cut with scissors along the line of dots until you reach the first mark made at the lowest point of the curve. Trim off the trailing excess paper that overlays the raised cheekpiece. Then turn the stock to lie on the off side once again, and position the paper on the cheekpiece side as before. Place a holding tape at the forward portion of the line just cut and another just shy of the ending point of the cut by the dot first made.

Now place marks along the base of the rear rounded portion of the curve that runs upward nearest the butt end of the stock, beginning at the center area of the stock and ending at its upper edge. Then remove the holding tapes from the forward portion, lift the paper, and cut it along the line of dots as before, trimming away the remaining excess from the top portion of the paper. Your pattern sheet should now be able to lie flat against the stock, with a long rear portion that you can roll over the top of the stock and secure to the opposite side. Once it is secured, make a light pencil mark along the inside edge of the buttplate and a parallel line $^{3}/_{8}$ to $^{1}/_{2}$ inch forward of the buttplate edge. If your paper reaches or extends beyond the pistol grip portion, you should also mark the upper line of curve of the ball-of-thumb, the recess, and the rear borderline of the checkering. Mark a full-length line on the paper along the center of the buttstock underside from buttplate to grip area, then make a light $^{1}/_{4}$-inch-long line on the cheekpiece side at each end of the pattern sheet at 1 inch from, and parallel with, the centerline-of-stock mark.

Place two such marks $^{3}/_{8}$ to $^{1}/_{2}$ inch rearward of the border of the checkering, one at the top and one at the bottom. You will use these $^{1}/_{4}$-inch lines (Figure L), in conjunction with the marks at the grip and butt areas, to outline the exact area open for carving. Slip an inch-long piece of masking tape half under the forward edge of the paper, and press it securely to the stock. Now draw a $^{1}/_{2}$-inch-long line half on the paper and half on the tape.

If your paper extends beyond the buttplate and fully covers the locator tape, trim the paper in place so that its edge only partially overlaps the tape, exposing enough tape on which to draw a locator mark but leaving sufficient paper to cover all of the stock where it meets the buttplate. This sometimes means trimming a half-round circle in the paper at the area of the tape. If for some reason this should not be possible, you will have to lift the paper, draw a locator mark in ink on the tape, and then trace this mark on the pattern sheet. This latter procedure is standard on several pattern layouts I have described later in the book.

After marking the locator tapes, place a full-length line along the rear edge of the buttstock at its meeting point with the buttplate. Then remove the pattern and connect the area lines using a pen and a straightedge.

Now you may trim away any excess paper beyond the extreme rear of the buttplate. The pattern sheet is trimmed along the rear edge of the buttplate in order to provide a more suitable edge for securing tapes during subsequent procedures. You're now ready to begin the actual woodwork. ★

# 16.

# Colored Front-Sight Inserts: A Better Method

*This alternative to the factory-installed, colored ramp-type sight blade works even with Patridge-type sights.*

*by Chip Todd*

**M**any new revolvers and pistols are sold with plastic front-sight inserts designed to make the front sight easier to pick up against varied backgrounds. The most popular color for these inserts seems to be red; thus, they are commonly called "red-ramp sights." For some reason, no one seems to have found a good way to use the factory-insert idea with Patridge-type front sights. In this report, I'll show you how to install my version of a sight insert—in any color you like.

The prevailing way to install this type of insert is with a dovetailed slot cut laterally in the ramped portion of the sight. This means that the insert does not reach the top of the blade, and is quite visible from the side. Moreover, the dovetailed insert doesn't lend itself to the Patridge-style sight blade, so there are no factory inserts for that blade. I determined early on that I didn't like the dovetail insert, which I consider an eyesore, so I designed one which is visible to the shooter, but only when viewed from the rear. As they say, "beauty is in the eye of the beerholder (uh, make that beholder)," so I don't expect everyone to like my version.

As a mechanical engineer working in mechanism and designs, my approach to an aesthetic redesign problem is to determine what I don't like about the looks of the existing product, and then try to visualize just the opposite. Since function is the most important thing about the sight, any new design must work at least as well as the original, and surpass it if possible.

I didn't like the dovetail look or the fact that the insert doesn't reach

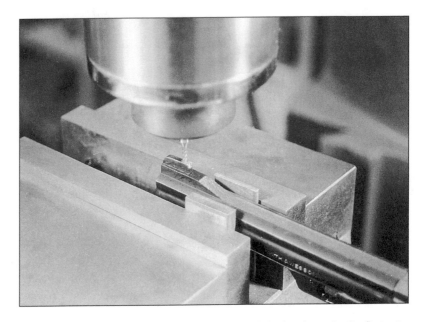

**Above:** *With the S&W Model 19 with Patridge sight in the vise, take the first cut to locate the end of the inletting for the plastic insert.*

to the highest point on the blade. To cure the first, I needed to leave the sides of the sight-blade intact, so I would have to do my inletting only on the ramped surface and the top of the blade. The second fault would automatically be cured if the inlet extended onto the top surface of the blade. This would be possible using a mill, with the end-mill cutter vertical and the cut made parallel to the bore. As this would leave the front end of the inlet radiused and the bottom of the cut square, I had to decide if this would be acceptable and esthetically pleasing. I could change either end of the cut by slanting the mill's head to an angle, making the front appear square, or the back rounded. I tried both on a Japanese plastic S&W Model 19 that I got from a friend in Japan, and settled on the square bottom and radiused front.

In checking through the handguns owned by my wife and me, I was surprised to find that we had no ramped sights that weren't already inserted by either the factory or me—except on a S&W model 34 (not a candidate), and a 6-inch model 19. As I didn't want to use a Patridge sight for the article, this meant that I would have to use a loose sight or one of the spare barrels I had collected. I had an S&W Model 19 barrel which was to go on a friend's gun, so I chose that to do the work for this article. I hope the fact that it is not mounted on a frame won't distract the reader from seeing the fine-looking insert.

While this can be done with a Dremel tool and a lot of courage, I wouldn't suggest trying this job without a milling machine. It just isn't easy to correct an errant cut when you are cutting a piece of metal as thin as this. I also feel that the lack of side-load-bearing "beef" on a drill press would make using a drill press risky, too. Patience, of which I am in short supply, can lessen the risk of using less-than-optimum equipment, so be your own judge. I used to use a hand drill for the anchor holes, but now use the mill for that as well.

Whether to serrate the finished insert or leave it smooth is also your decision, but be forewarned: Serrating does add some additional risk if you are heavy-handed. The file I used to serrate the insert to match the S&W ramp serrations is the 40-lpi metal-checkering file from Brownells.

I use a 5/64-inch-diameter end-mill cutter for the Smith &Wesson's 1/8-inch-wide front blade. This leaves about a .023 inch thickness of metal on each side—enough to contain the insert. I recommend a four-fluted high-speed steel cutter. I use the four-flute to reduce the vibrations and high-speed steel for its cleaner cut. I also buy stub-length cutters so there will be less tendency for the bit to flex or wander around. A slow feed will help to insure that the cutter won't flex from the side forces exerted by the leading flute.

A good layer of masking tape on each side of the barrel will protect the finish from the parallel bars. This is the easiest of the protection methods that I use; I always use brass shimstock or old letterpress Linotype lead pieces for non-slip padding. I also keep some thin lead sheeting around, having been in the x-ray industry for a while, but I never use it on a rounded surface that is to be clamped, as the pressure could make the barrel mash through the thin lead. Since I am quite partial to the S&W Model 19 and 66 revolvers, I have milled a couple of lead ingots that fit each side of a 19's barrel and fit around the ejector shroud. These do quite a good job of protection, and they help me get the revolver in a perfectly vertical position without even trying.

If the milling vise you are going to use isn't high enough above the mill's table to allow the barrel to be horizontal without the butt interfering, then it might be necessary to do some trickery in clamping the barrel into the vise. I often use some of my parallel bars (which are taller than the mill vise jaws) to do this by using a sliding parallel bar to duplicate the thickness of the barrel at the bottom of the vertical bars, the milling vise jaws in the middle, and the barrel at the top.

When the barrel is captured in the vise, I level it with an electronic level, only because I have one; a bubble level will do just as well. Then, I put a hardened steel pin in the milling collet to check that the sight

**Above:** *Shown here is the finished inletting for the plastic insert in a Patridge (target) sight. Note the oil splatter, which must be cleaned off before filling the inlet with plastic compound.*

blade is vertical, or, better yet, use the level against the side of the frame or the gripframe to do this more accurately.

You can use the hard stops provided on the milling table to keep you from going too far in cutting the inlet for the insert. Since I have digital readouts on mine, I now just do it by number. Regardless of how you do it, it's necessary to put some kind of limit on the cut, as the cutter is quite small in diameter and the last few cuts will be at a depth of almost 1/4 inch in steel. I have found that setting the hard stop is best done on the first cut (about .02 inch deep) by snugging the stop slightly and letting the mill push it to where you want it to stop. I would then back up and tighten up the stop, repeating the cut at the same depth to prove out the stop.

If you are not familiar with cutting with this size of end mill cutter, I would suggest that some cutting be done in scrap steel so that you can become accustomed to the metal and can prove out the cutter speed that you are thinking of using. This will also give you a chance to get familiar with the feed rate that will work best. On this small a cutter, I try to feed at as slow a rate as I can make myself work (which is usually not really as slow as I should), and use plenty of cutting fluid. I think that the old sulfurated cutting oil is as good as any at that price, but I'm allergic to sulfur, so I use more expensive MicroFinish oil or a tapping/cutting fluid.

As mentioned earlier, we have the choice of having the ends of the insert rounded or squared, and, to have anything but rounded on top and square on the bottom, the head of the mill, or the angle of the barrel, must be changed. Since it is easier to change the angle of the barrel in the mill vise, that's what I'd suggest if you want another combination. As I've always liked the barrel level and the cutter vertical, I just make the inlet like that. I'm sure you can imagine how the top cut would come out with a square top surface if the last cut was with the barrel slanted, muzzle downward and a light cut only at the top was made.

I start my inletting with about a .02-inch-deep cut, set the stop or note the digital readout, and continue making successive cuts about .02 inch deep. By the time I get down to the base of the sight blade, the cut is large enough to need about "two and a half BB's" worth's of filling material to fill it. My last cut is done quite slowly, as are any slight cleaning cuts needed to smooth the sides of the cut. I find that these extra cuts are needed more often when using a mill/drill instead of the more rigid knee mill.

**Above:** Drilling two small retaining holes in the bottom of the inletting allows "pegs" to form, which bind the plastic insert into the inlet.

**Above:** *Here, the ramped front-sight blade has copper-shim dams clamped on each side to help contain the casting compound. Clockwise from behind the clamp are four pigment containers, the solvent bottle, opened resin powder container, spatula, stick, dropper, and mixing bowl.*

As with any dovetailed insert, small anchoring pegs should be angled out from the insert to insure that it can't be jarred or pulled loose from the inlet. This is somewhat easier on a dovetailed insert, as the holes which form the pegs can be drilled vertically. With two directions that a hidden insert can escape from the inletting, I find myself wanting two peg holes at angles which differ. This prevents the insert flying out in a direction axial to either of the pegs, as the other peg prevents this.

I use an automatic center punch to make two little indentions in the inside of the inlet, one on the front wall and the other on the bottom of the inlet. I use as large a diameter drill bit as I can without hitting either sidewall of the inlet, as I want to insure that the insert material will flow down into the drill holes or can be easily poked in with a toothpick. For this, I use a 1/16-inch bit in a 1/4-inch hand drill. The "peg holes" only need be about .05 inch deep, as their job is in shear and not much is needed at an angle.

After the peg holes are drilled, I clean away any oil residue left from the machining with trichloroethane. (I know. But can you think of anything that *doesn't* give laboratory rats cancer when fed to them in massive quantities?) Use rubbing alcohol, if you prefer. Just de-grease it well.

There are many choices of sight insert compounds. It's simply an acrylic powder and solvent like dentists use. The one I use the most is the Bullshooter's brand that I buy from Brownells, but have also had good results with Lee's Red Ramp material.

Since most of the rear sights are matte black, it would seem logical to use a contrasting color in the front sight. Of course, a shooter who is red-green colorblind should think more in terms of contrasting shades and stay away from red. I have used white, but have found it hard to avoid contamination, causing specks to appear. These specks are either particles that got into the stuff as I was mixing it, or steel particles induced from the final filing of the blade. Fluorescent green contrasts well, but disappears against leaves—and who wants a green sight, anyway? If the insert is going into a stainless-steel front blade, I would use a dark color and make the inlet slightly thinner to give a silver wall on each side of the insert. Everybody has a preference, so just follow your instincts. I have kept several combinations in demo "dummies" in my shop for years, so that they could be tried against different backgrounds. It's hard to go wrong with the fluorescent red.

I confine the compound in the area by clamping a thin, brass shim on each side of the sight blade, using a parallel-jawed clamp. Absolute damming isn't exactly necessary, as the stuff is easy to take off with a

*Above:* This photo shows a clamped sight blade with a small bit of fluorescent red compound added to patch up a tiny pinhole void in the plastic. A "wet" mixture is needed to fill in tiny voids.

**Above:** *The guns on the left have factory red-and-black dovetail inserts. The guns on the right have red-and-white ramp and Patridge sight inserts done according to the technique outlined in the text. Note that neither of the sight inserts on the right-hand guns can be seen from the sides of the firearm, but they are fully visible to the shooter.*

fingernail after the dams come off and before it reaches full hardness. I do, however, try to get the shim material flat and against the sides of the blade. Be sure to get the clamp as far out of the way as you can, because some of the insert compounds don't allow you much time to play around. You'll have to take some time to tamp some of the compound down into the peg holes with a toothpick, so think ahead to avoid anything that takes unnecessary time.

Mixing the compound varies from one brand to another, so it would behoove you to read that particular manufacturer's directions. If the compound is a powder and the solvent is a thin, volatile liquid, I put the resin powder in a shallow mixing container like a contact-lens case, and add the solvent with a dropper while stirring with a thin spatula. I have found that there is a fine line between having the mixture too thick and too thin. Get it so that it will just barely flow, so that it will be easier to get into the peg-holes. If it is too thin, it will be hard to contain and it will shrink so that there will be a "sinkhole" in the center of the insert.

For brands of insert material which have white resin powder, put the solvent into the mixing container first, add a small dot of color, and stir them quickly. Then sprinkle in the resin powder a little at a time while stirring. When the mixture just starts to take on a slightly granular look, stop with the powder. This should be about right to tamp into the peg-holes and heap up between the shim pieces.

If the mixture is of two pastes, then mix the resin and color, and then put in the solvent. Caution; the color paste goes a long way, so you only have to put a small dot of it on a toothpick and stir it into the resin.

I usually apply insert material with a tapered flexible-steel spatula, but sometimes I break out the polycarbonate spatula, especially if I am having to work with a light color. Heap the insert mix between the dams, up slightly above the blade, and tamp it as well as you can. Sometimes, if I have misjudged the mixture, I add about a half drop of the solvent to the top of the heap, but be careful when you do this not to dissolve the whole thing.

As mentioned before, patience is my weak suit, so I usually dry the insert material with a 60- or 100-watt light bulb for about 10 minutes. I let it sit another 15 minutes, and then feel good about working on it. I only do any filing after I have poked on the insert with an X-Acto knife blade to check if it's hard enough to file without crumbling. It should give a slick, not crystalline surface when filed.

When the insert is hard enough, I remove the shim dams by rotating the shims to slide them away—not by pulling them to the sides. Any excess compound on the outside of the sight blade is usually easy to scrape away with a fingernail. Wait at least another 30 minutes or so before filing—or overnight if possible. Then, if the insert is hard, have at it.

The files I use for this are very fine, so it is essential that the teeth be cleaned quite often during the filing process. Use very soft file strokes and, whenever possible, file along the blade, and not across it, as this can cause the thin sidewalls of the inlet to separate from the compound. Filing along the blade, and not across, will lessen the possibility of this. File the insert down flat until the metal on each side of it is filed also. This metal can be cold blued quite easily (if it's not stainless).

You may want to leave the insert with a plain, slick surface, but if there are serrations already on the rear surface of the ramp, then it usually looks better to continue the serrations across the insert. The serrations on most S&W handguns are of a 40-lines-per-inch pattern, and they can be easily restored with a metal-checkering file of that number. Serrating the insert will, necessarily, have to align with the existing serrations, so the first few strokes need to be guided by those already there. This will insure that the serrations on the insert will coincide with those left on the top of the metal walls on each side of the insert.

Serrating need be done with very light strokes which aren't deep enough or under enough pressure to bend the sides of the sight blade's inletting. The filing with the checkering file must continue until the serrations in the insert match the original serrations on the sight blade.

When the serrations meet my approval, I usually spray the insert with trichloroethane and use a toothbrush to clean out the serrations before bluing. Be sure to blow whatever solvent you use to clean the area, as most bluing compounds don't work well if anything is still on the metal.

I have found that Brownells Oxpho-Blue doesn't stain most insert materials, so I reblue carbon-steel sight blades that have been filed or serrated with this bluing compound. I wouldn't try any paste-type bluing without first testing it on some of the material used for the insert.

After the bluing has been rinsed off and the area saturated with water-displacing oil and wiped again, test view the insert against the rear blade's notch in the same type of lighting you expect to encounter when shooting.

If the color of the insert is less than desirable, it's fairly easy to dig it out with a Dremel tool and replace it with another color. I have found that the fluorescent red almost always pleases me, and I trust you'll find the same to be true with the sights you do. ★

# 17.

# Gunsmithing Concealed-Carry Guns

*When optimizing a gun for concealed carry, less is sometimes better—think of yourself as a police armorer rather than a gunsmith.*

*by Chick Blood*

A research report from the University of Chicago recently stated with certainty that crime was down in states with right-to-carry laws. Proclaiming the research to be flawed, the anti-gun crowd—Schumer, Brady, and that bunch—received far more press coverage than the report. Attorney General Janet Reno declined comment because she "hadn't read the research."

No mention was made by the anti-gunners or the media of two other documents which preceded the Chicago research. The first was a press release issued by the Federal Bureau of Investigation which summarized the Justice Department's Preliminary Annual Uniform Crime Report for 1995. The release stated that crimes reported to all law-enforcement agencies dropped by 2 percent in 1995 compared to 1994. Geographically, the release continued, there were decreases in violent and property crime in all regions except the West, where property crime remained at the 1994 level. Cities with over 1,000,000 population experienced the largest decline in their overall crime index of 6 percent. A 1-percent increase occurred in cities with 500,000 to 999,999 inhabitants and in cities with fewer than 25,000. Suburban counties showed a 1-percent decrease in crime levels; rural counties a 3-percent increase.

After reading the press release, I wanted to know whether crime had decreased more in the 30 states with right-to-carry laws, compared to states that have not yet adopted such laws. I called the FBI, and was referred to the Bureau of Justice Statistics. A lengthy recorded message there led me to the National Criminal Justice Service, where I was greeted by another recorded message telling me that all their lines were busy.

**Above:** *Introduced in 1994, the Kahr K9 has gained significant popularity because of its ability to handle full-power 9mm loads.*

I heard the same message the next day, and for several days after that. Eventually, I turned to other sources that had proven to be equally reliable. That's where the second document mentioned earlier was uncovered.

Apparently, FBI data for 1994 shows that, compared to states still clinging to more restrictive gun laws, states with right-to-carry laws had a 21-percent-lower overall violent crime rate, a 27-percent-lower firearm violent crime rate, a 28-percent-lower homicide rate, a 33-percent-lower firearm homicide rate, a 35-percent-lower firearm robbery rate, a 15-percent-lower aggravated assault rate, and an 18-percent-lower firearm aggravated assault rate.

Nearly 120 million Americans who have been granted the right to carry a handgun. More millions have expectations of joining them in the future. What kind of gun are they most likely to carry? And what are they most likely to ask of you when it comes to servicing it?

## Which Handgun and Why?

Try hiding a Desert Eagle, Red Hawk, or S&W Model 29 under a suit coat, or a sports jacket. Sure, it's possible; if you have a good tailor and don't mind walking funny. Nevertheless, light, compact revolvers and semi-autos that are easy to secret on the person or in a purse are the firearms of choice among those who choose to carry concealed. The most popular calibers are .22, .25, .38, .380, and 9mm, with the .40 S&W gaining ground as compact handguns chambered for it reach the market.

The only thing more important than size is reliability. Absolute reliability. In that respect, concealed-carry firearms are kissing cousins to law-enforcement duty weapons. Their purpose is identical: to prevent, to control, or—under the most desperate of circumstances—to kill. Like most law-enforcement arms, few of them will ever be employed for the latter. As a deterrent or means of control, however, the mere suspicion of their presence has been and is being widely credited with contributing to declining crime rates. That's arguable in some circles. This isn't one of them.

So, we have size and we have reliability. The gunsmith has little if anything to do with one, and everything to do with the other.

## Modifications to Consider...And to Avoid

A wise gunsmith will not make the sort of alterations commonly performed on handguns used in competitions to a handgun intended for concealed carry. In fact, anyone asking for such changes should be

**Above:** *The Lady Smith descended from the Model 60 Chief's Special. The revolver started life as a .38 S&W Special, but is now offered in .357 Magnum as well.*

talked out of making them.

For example, target trigger jobs are out. Too light a pull can result in misfires, particularly in double-action revolvers. In pistols packing full loads, overly light pulls and uncontrollable bursts of full-automatic fire are synonymous.

On the other hand, smooth trigger pulls are in. Even a heavy trigger can be made to feel lighter and more comfortable with a simple polishing job. Underscore "polishing." Make no changes in sear-engagement angles or hammer-notch depths, and pay great attention to internal details—details like the sides of the hammer, the interior of the frame, and the hammer-spring strut on pistols or revolvers that employ them. Don't overlook anything that could cause drag on the gun's firing mechanism.

If and when parts are needed, replace them with factory parts—unless you're sure that the aftermarket parts you choose meet factory specs. Doing otherwise might be argued in court as an "unauthorized modification." Should an injury to the shooter or an innocent person result, you could be held accountable. And keep in mind that securing factory parts for many imported handguns can be difficult if not impossible.

Most defensive shooting takes place at a range of 7 yards or less. At that distance, the need for pinpoint accuracy does not reach critical proportions. In other words, 95 percent of the accuracy-enhancing add-ons available for competition handguns are unnecessary—even undesirable—in a carry weapon. One such device I receive many requests for, from civilians and law enforcement officers alike, is a laser aiming device. In the first place, I tell them, it adds bulk to the gun even when built-in. In the second, third, and fourth places,

***Above left and right:*** *Before and after "bobbing" photos of a Colt .38 Lightweight revolver. The first cut can be made with a hacksaw. Finishing is by grinding wheel or file, followed by polishing and touch-up bluing, if required. When grinding, use caution to avoid overheating the part and destroying the temper.*

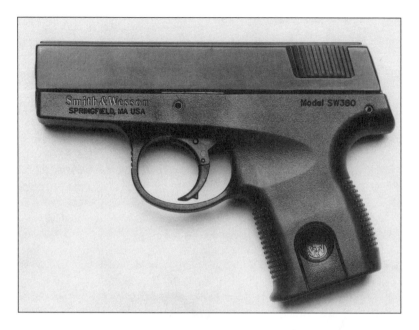

**Above:** *The Sigma Series SW380 is the first semi-auto chambered for the .380 ACP, which was introduced by John Browning in 1908 for the Colt Pocket Automatic. The "Baby Sigma" has a polymer frame, steel slide, stainless-steel barrel, and a striker-driven ignition system.*

a laser is rendered useless by rain, fog, snow, smoke, or dust, and can become an aiming point for an adversary. Aside from that, I'm all in favor of intimidating little red dots.

Continuing on the same subject, sights on carry weapons should be rugged, firmly anchored, and small but easily acquired. So called "night sights" with radiant front and rear elements are perfectly acceptable, and are manufactured for most handguns. Adjustable rears, if insisted upon, can be installed. Just make sure that the sight doesn't extend too far outward from the sides of the slide or top strap to avoid the possibility of snagging on clothing when the gun is drawn. Similar snags can happen with front sights when they are too high.

## Autoloader Improvements

If the gun is a few years old or of foreign manufacture, its magazine well is likely to be squared off with sharp edges at the opening. This can catch on a magazine that's not perfectly centered in the well when inserted under duress. Being extremely careful not to thin out the frame,

**Left:** *Outfitting someone with a holster adds value to your gunsmithing service. You should emphasize getting the most comfortable rig possible.*

the edges of the well can be beveled at 45 degrees to provide more positive insertion of a misaligned magazine. The beveling can be accomplished by hand, but is more accurately done with a milling machine, with the work locked in at the correct angle. A cutter or grinding point can be used to create the bevel, after which the metal should be polished. If the gun is blue, you'll have some touching up to do.

The feed ramp of any self-loader should be polished. By hand. A piece of fine emery cloth wrapped around a dowel can remove machine marks and rough spots very nicely. Polish the result with crocus cloth and dowel. With the same rig, polish the throat of the barrel which, hopefully, is already throated—or opened up—to improve feeding. If it isn't, the gun probably wasn't made in the U.S.—not recently anyway. Don't risk throating a foreign-made stranger or any unthroated barrel on which "how to" information isn't readily available. Content yourself with polishing what throat exists, and advise the owner to restrict the ammo used to full-jacketed roundnose. They're just begging for jams with hollowpoint or truncated bullets anyway, since many small-caliber autoloaders simply aren't made to swallow them.

Generally, the grip stocks of pistols need no replacement, unless they have a thumb rest or are made of rubber. Thumb rests serve no purpose in defensive shooting and tend to interfere with a two-handed grip. Rubber grip stocks often cling to a coat, revealing the fact that a gun is being carried. There are pros and cons to tipping off others, hostile or otherwise, to the presence of a gun. But if the objective is to carry concealed, get rid of the rubber grips.

In addition, avoid the installation of extended slide-release levers. With a two-hand grip, the shooter doesn't need an extended slide release. Besides, some of them are so big they can put a nasty rip in a shirt or jacket when the gun is drawn. When they get really hung up, the gun can't be drawn at all, which kind of defeats the idea of carrying one in the first place.

Single-action-only and combined DA/SA pistols can come out of the box with a hammer wearing a spur. In many cases, the manufacturer will have bobbed hammers available. If so, a bobbed version should be installed, or the existing hammer bobbed, for the reasons discussed in the next section.

## Improvements to Double-Action Revolvers

The spur on a hammer can be of great assistance to someone trying to wrench a gun out of your hand. The person doing the wrenching may receive a painful puncture wound in the process, but pain is dulled by many things—not the least of which are drugs, booze, and the all-consuming drive to steal the money to buy them. The likelihood of a revolver being taken away from its owner—and possibly turned against that owner—can be reduced by bobbing the hammer. The thumb piece can be completely removed or mostly removed and radiused. Lopping it off can be done with a bench grinder, a fine-tooth hacksaw, or a metal-cutting wheel. Finishing is by file, stone, and crocus cloth.

A post-type front sight can also offer a similar handhold to an opponent. It should be reshaped, or "ramped," to slope to the rear, making it easier to yank the barrel out of an adversary's grasp. The same modification helps keep a firearm from getting stuck in its holster.

In stressful situations, a finger on a grooved or serrated trigger tends to push or pull a gun off target. Primarily, this happens because the finger is pretty much wrapped around the trigger, not merely touching it just above the first joint as in bullseye shooting. The solution is to grind or file off the trigger grooves and polish it out.

**Above:** *This revolver trigger has had the finger grooves ground off; a smooth trigger helps prevent "pushing" or "pulling" the gun off target in high-stress conditions.*

Unlike pistols, the grip stocks on many revolvers can be on the bulky side. If the original manufacturer doesn't offer options, it is perfectly acceptable to replace them with more compact or more rounded ones chosen from the aftermarket. Grips with finger grooves, for example, are highly desirable in defensive shooting and are available from a number of reliable sources including Brownells, Pachmayr, and Hogue.

## Handguns Designed To Be Carried

Only three are shown here, but there are dozens of different models available both imported and domestic. Because they have been built specifically for concealed carry, there are no sharp edges; their sights are already suited to their task; and hammer spurs, if any, are held to minimal lengths, as you can see with the Lady Smith Model 60LS. Incidentally, the Lady Smith .38 Special was introduced in 1990 after evolving from the Model 60 Chief's Special of 1965.

The Kahr K9 has no long list of distinguished ancestors like the Lady Smith. It was introduced just two years ago at the 1994 Shooting, Hunting, and Outdoor Trade (SHOT) Show as the only subcompact capable of firing any commercially manufactured, full-powered 9mm round including +P. The K9 measures 6 inches in length and 4.5 inches in height, and will be no larger in caliber .40 S&W, its newest incarnation. By the way, the hand pictured holding the pistol doesn't belong to a giant. Actually, it's pretty average in size. I know that for sure because it's mine.

A closer examination of the photo showing the Model SW380 Sigma reveals a design that echoes everything stated here about concealed-carry handguns. Its front and rear sights are integral parts of the ramp atop its slide, and the rest of the gun isn't square—anywhere. Even the slide's cocking serrations are slightly radiused. We'll be covering the Sigma in more detail in a later issue, but there are a couple of things worth bringing up right now. A dry slide is just about this gun's worst enemy. Make sure it's nice and slick by lubricating it with a Teflon impregnated grease. Another thing, after 1,500 to 2,500 rounds, depending on how "dirty" the ammo, remove the slide's end cap and flush out the striker recess. The cap is removed with the slide upside down on the bench. There's a little plastic collar just ahead of the rear of the striker. Reach in with a small punch and push the collar—it's in a small depression—toward the front of the slide. This takes the spring pressure off the end cap so it can be pushed down with the thumb. The spring you compressed may escape, along with some firing-pin-assembly parts, if you don't keep it under control when the end cap clears.

## Conclusion

When a concealed-carry handgun is brought in for gunsmithing, it may be helpful to try to forget you're a gunsmith. Instead, approach the job as if you were a police armorer working on a duty weapon. In these cases, that's exactly what you're doing. No more. No less. ★

# 18.

# Polishing Metal: Prep Prior To Bluing

*If you can't stand the chemistry, get a bluing service to protect your metalwork. But save yourself money by preparing the metal first.*

**B**luing is one area of gunsmithing that is seeing increasing specialization. Many companies and individuals are taking on this metal-finishing role ,which few of us enjoy performing, but which is certainly necessary. One way in which we can get this noxious work done—but still maintain a cost savings—is to send bluing specialists metalwork that has already been prepared. Doing your own disassembly also adds to the cost reduction. Hobbyists can also save some bucks on the restoration of an older gun that junior will need for his first deer season by learning how to prepare the metal for bluing.

*By Dennis A. Wood*

## Step One

There are several ways to remove rust and old bluing. Sanding is one common option, but it's not the best solution.

Rust and bluing remover is inexpensive, and it doesn't carry the danger of rubbing off serial numbers and manufacturer names like sanding. A liquid rust remover works better to get into the nooks and crannies often encountered on firearms. Birchwood Casey and Brownells both offer bluing remover in a liquid form, and there is even a gel type available.

You need only have the solution and a section off a roll of thick paper towels soaked in bluing remover to get started.

Bluing remover will only work when dealing with steel parts. (If you want to refinish any aluminum parts that were previously anodized, a whole different set of rules apply.) The rubbing needs to be done several times until the solution begins to cut through the skin of old bluing, but keep at it. It will come off.

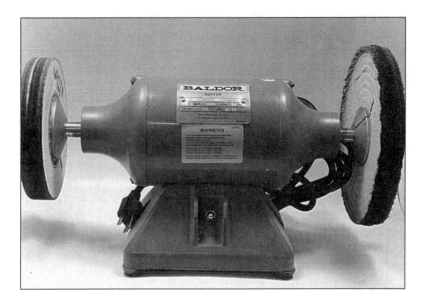

**Above:** *The Baldor buffer runs much more smoothly than washing-machine motors.*

Once all the bluing has been removed from the metal, you should be looking at a dull, gray-colored, firearm. Rinse the metal with as hot a water as you can stand, and then dry it thoroughly with more towels or compressed air.

All the flaws that got you started refinishing this gun should now be quite visible, and you'll probably discover a few you didn't know were there.

## Step Two

Polishing can get as elaborate as you desire or as simple. A reputable job can be performed with emery paper and a small rubber sanding block. Rust, if it has progressed to the pitting stage, can require a lot of rubbing with the emery paper. If the pits are excessively deep, removing them completely may not be a good idea. Thinning the metal excessively may compromise safety in some areas. If you have a firearm with deep pits, my recommendation is to go with a glass bead or sandblast finish prior to the bluing. This will produce a matte finish with less light reflection and hold oil better to prevent any future rust problems. This is sometimes referred to as a hunter finish and is gaining in popularity with experienced hunters who know how shiny guns can spook game.

Tool marks can be quite obvious on a barrel when dealing with military-issue firearms, and if the desire to smooth these ridges exists, #220 grit emery paper would be good to start with. Wrap the #220 grit paper around the barrel and start cutting in long, even strokes, striving to apply equal pressure as you go. The idea is not to dwell in one area too long. Go easy around barrel markings. If you encounter raised burrs such as those found around tapped front or rear sight holes, a smooth-cut file lightly drawn across these burrs will get them down to barrel diameter. At the junction of the barrel and receiver a shoe-shine motion will allow the paper to get up-close to the shoulder more easily.

Whenever flat areas are encountered, some sort of a sanding block is in order. Whether it be plastic, rubber, or a hardwood block, it is much easier to maintain flatness if a sanding block is used, especially when going around and over pin or screw holes. These areas can get dished out quite quickly if a block is not used and ruin the look of your refinishing job. Radiused areas can give fits when trying to maintain the original contour without a backup for the emery paper. Wood dowels make for a good enough sanding block when getting into these areas. If you want to go one step further, stop by your automotive parts store and get as many different diameters of car hose as you can. Insert a wood dowel of appropriate diameter into the hose for stiffness and make the overall length about 1 to 2 inches. The hose rubber keeps

**Above:** *Felt wheels for the grinder, charged with #400 grit rouge, will give a factory finish to the metal.*

the emery paper from sliding around and is stiff enough to get the job done when getting into radiused areas. These little round sanding blocks come in handy when doing stock work also.

Progress with the next step up in finer grit emery paper until you get the desired look you are after. Most factory finishes are done to a #400 grit. Emery paper can be had in #220, #280, #320, #360, #400, #600, #800, and #1200 grit and probably a few in between that I missed. I'm not too fond of mirror-type finishes because they are gaudy and oil has a tendency to slide off the surface rather than stay in place and do its intended job. Also, fingerprints seem to show up more visibly on mirror finishes, and some people seem to have more acid or salt in their paws than others, causing a problem if they are not removed quickly.

## Power Polishing

I can't remember how many years I struggled with discarded washing machine motors that were employed to run a buffing wheel. It seems that whenever I got an old motor the driving shaft would not run true. Of course, the buffing wheel would not run true as a result of shaft run-out, so wheel break-in time always seemed to take forever. Then, trying to polish a part with an elliptically rotating wheel can make your patience run out real fast, let alone scouting around for the part that the wheel knocked out of your hand.

***Above:*** *Sanding blocks should always back emery paper to maintain contours.*

**Above:** *Abrasive or glass beads will give a matte look with less glare.*

To solve these problems, I finally purchased a Baldor buffing machine. This machine looks like a bench grinder and runs at 3600 rpm. Wheel break-in time is a lot shorter, and it runs very smoothly. If you plan on doing polishing on a long term basis at least give the Baldor buffing machine some consideration.

Both the right and left shafts on this buffer are ¹/₂ inch in diameter, and the machine is rated at ¹/₃ horsepower. Thus, 6-inch buffing wheels work best. There is plenty of written advice on the proper methods of machine buffing, so I'll just deal with what works for me. For roughing work started with #120 and then #240 grit rouge, I use spiral stitched sisal wheels, three 6 by ¹/₂-inch wheels mounted side by side. Getting into #320 grit and finer the soft felt wheels get the call to duty. Medium and hard felt wheels are used for the #500 series of rouges for the finer finishes some folks desire. Being that I have only one buffer I place a black witness mark on the wheel along with grit size and rotation direction so that when switching to different wheels it is easier to align them for true running. It is always best to use one size grit for a particular wheel. Never use more than one grit on a wheel or you will defeat the progressive sequence of polishing. When not in immediate use these wheels are stored in plastic Zip-Lock bags to prevent any contamination by an errant particles. Follow the instructions for storing your rouges properly. I use the Polish-O-Ray products sold through Brownells mainly because they work well and I can get most of the stuff I need from that one source.

## Step Three

After you have successfully polished your firearm to whatever finish was chosen, the metal will need to be protected during shipment to the person doing the bluing. The biggest problem: rust. The solution: Any good protecting oil or grease swabbed liberally onto the metal will protect it. Cellophane wrap of the type used to wrap food leftovers will work to keep the oil on the metal in transit and your bluing service will be happy to see it rust free when it arrives.

## Alternative Finishes

Gaining popularity is the matte-type metal finishes put in place prior to bluing. The equipment needed is usually an air compressor, blasting gun and the particular size glass beads or grit to get the desired amount of matte. By using some creative masking with tape, two-tone finishes can be achieved. Matte finishes are less prone to reflect sunlight, and the rougher surface will retain oil when the firearm is stored during the off season. On badly pitted guns, sandblasting is about the only means of getting the rust thoroughly out of the pits, and once blued, the pits are not as noticeable. ★

# 19.

# Cold Bluing
# Tips and Techniques

*While not as good as a hot-blue job, sometimes*
*cold bluing is necessary. Here are some*
*ways to get the right finish.*

*by Chip Todd*

Anyone can discolor metal, but it takes effort and care to get a cold-blued finish of which you can be proud. First, recognize the fact that no method of cold bluing can match the durability and beauty of a hot-bluing job done by an experienced gun refinisher. Bluing is the final state of the oxidation process of steel, and requires very caustic chemicals and heat to penetrate the metal surface deeply. In short, it takes money; a well-ventilated room; and a will to fight city hall, the EPA, and OSHA to have a decent hot-bluing operation.

The main difference between hot bluing and cold bluing is in the salts that are used. For hot bluing, alkaline salts are used at approximately 290 degrees Fahrenheit, while most cold-bluing solutions are acidic and used at room temperature. A third method of bluing is called Nitre bluing which is almost neutral, but must be used above 540 degrees Fahrenheit. I won't touch on the Nitre-bluing process here, as it is used to a much lesser degree than the other two. The boundary "ring or haze" you have gotten when trying to touch up factory bluing is caused by the neutral area formed between the two types of bluing. This is why it can be so hard to get the "invisible" spot touch-up job.

The advantages of the cold-bluing method are apparent when one checks out the prices of heated tanks, the inherent dangers of dealing with caustic and/or hot chemicals, and the great difficulty in disposing of depleted or dirty chemicals. My favorite bluing craftsman has his setup next to his swimming pool as a safety precaution in case he gets seriously splashed with the caustic solution. I didn't want to use caustic chemicals around my children when they were young, and I have

**Above:** These are the primary tools you'll need to start a cold-bluing project.

since seen no reason to change. Therefore, I suggest leaving the hot solutions to the experienced gunsmiths who are used to dealing with the harsh chemicals, and who are willing to put up with rigid EPA requirements.

"Murphy's Law" of rebluing: The results are inversely proportional to the cost of the firearm, added to the pickiness of the owner. Remember, you will probably be dealing with someone who has no idea of the difficulty of your task; he thinks you just "dip it."

Now that I've shown why you might opt for the less durable cold bluing, let's get into how you can get reasonable results with some consistency. To do the work you have to have a high-interest level, a garage-type shop, and an adequate source of clean water.

## Suggested Equipment

To get started in cold bluing, I suggest you have the following equipment on hand:

- Small stainless-steel or polyethylene mixing bowl
- Plastic rectangular container (Tupperware type, pistol size)
- Face shield/eye protection
- Apron (chemical resistant)

- Cotton gloves (latex gloves usually leave prints in the finish)
- Dremel or other rotary grinder
- Forceps, tweezers, or clamps
- Good lighting

The following equipment is not necessary, but it will make the work easier and more trouble free:

- Air pressure and nozzle
- Scotchbrite wheel and/or buffing wheel
- Sandblasting or bead-blasting equipment

## Supplies

The supplies you will need include:

- Cotton swabs, Q-tips, clean rags
- Oil (water displacing)
- Bluing chemical
- Water, fresh & running, if possible
- Vinegar (white) or dilute muriatic acid
- Cratex wheels or lots of elbow grease
- XXXX steel wool
- Sandpaper (320, 400, and 600 grit)
- Scotchbrite pads

There are some things you shouldn't use at all, including newspapers, because the ink has residual chemicals which may ruin the results of your labors. And don't use WD-40 or other rust-preventing oils because they will eat away bluing.

## The Cold Bluing Process

The first thing you should do is inspect the gun you're going to work on for scratches, dents, and dings, which will have to be removed during the rebluing process. (I used a revolver for this demonstration.) Decide how they will affect the appearance of the finished pistol, and discuss with the owner whether the gun should be glossy or matte (dull). Glossy finishes tend to draw one's eye to the defects and are sure to displease the owner if these defects are more prominent than before he brought the piece to you. The answer is often to make selected parts matte and others glossy. This also calls for the owner's concurrence before proceeding.

Gloss is usually obtained by buffing the metal to a chrome-like surface, but this can be done manually if one has the time and energy to spare. In such a case, use finer and finer grit sandpaper until you reach 600 grit, and then polish with a good metal polish, such as SimiChrome polish (found at most motorcycle shops). Parts requiring a dull finish will need to be bead-blasted, sandblasted (extreme cases), or dulled with Scotchbrite pads. I find that the maroon-colored Scotchbrite pads are about like 320-grit sandpaper and work fairly well for this. (These are also good for taking out scratches on brushed stainless-steel guns.) Most of the interior parts will not need to be blued; it's only done when I think the owner won't take care in oiling the weapon at regular intervals.

Disassemble the firearm and store the parts that don't need bluing. I use a Seal-A-Meal machine which seals the parts in a plastic bag where they can't get easily lost. The parts which are to be blued are then degreased with Trichlorethylene 1,1,1 or other such degreaser. A handy source of this chemical is Berryman's Brake Cleaner which comes in a spray can from your local auto-parts store. Granted, this isn't the most economical form of degreasing, but it certainly is handy.

After the decision of dull vs. gloss has been made, you will either buff and polish the gun and parts, or bead-blast it to a satin gray. Be sure to tape off the surfaces with masking tape that don't show and shouldn't be roughened up before blasting the pieces. I also suggest you blast the receiver with the sideplate in place, as it is easier to obtain an evenness between pieces. I chose the matte finish for this article because it is the one that I'd recommend for one's first bluing job. The only difference in difficulty between the two finishes is that it's harder to get a grease-free metal surface after buffing with the waxy compound. The heat generated by buffing causes the wax to permeate the metal, and the wax is more difficult to remove than the glass powder from bead-blasting.

The main cause of most cold-bluing miseries is the lack of proper and complete degreasing of the parts. Even degreasers, which seem to have taken all of the grease from a part, usually fail to get all of the contaminants out of the pores of the metal. Formula 409 cleaner seemed to be the answer for a while, but I got several bad jobs in a row and started the search for something better. It just wouldn't get the worse cases of grease out and was useless against rust pits.

Firearms that have pitting will always need an acid bath in order to get the rust out of the pits. I've found I can get most contaminants and rust out of the metal by using either white vinegar (acetic acid) or dilute muriatic acid (hydrochloric acid). Soak stubborn parts in a very weak muriatic acid solution for about 30 minutes. Always pour the acid slowly into the water, *not* the water into the acid. You must also keep an eye on the part while it's soaking, as you don't want this process to eat any of the metal away, just get the rust and grease out of the pores. The part will develop an etched, gray surface, but this will not affect the gloss, unless taken to an extreme. The acid bath leaves the metal susceptible to immediate rusting (three minutes or less), so you must use caution and be observant, lest you have to replace an owner's favorite gun. When you see the gun emitting a host of small bubbles while in the acid bath, don't be alarmed that the metal is getting eaten away in a rush. The acid is just breaking down the glass powder that is in the pores of the metal from bead- or sandblasting. While the workpiece is in the acid bath, you may want to spend that time getting your bluing setup ready.

There are several good types and brands of bluing chemicals. Among them are Birchwood Casey's PermaBlue or SuperBlue; and Brownells' Dicropan IM, Oxpho-Blue, Dicropan T-4, and G-96 Gun Blue. Although any of these will give excellent results, for this article, I used Brownells Oxpho-Blue, as I have had good results with this for quite a few years.

Pour the bluing liquid into the bowl that you will use, and place it and some clean swabs on a clean area of your workbench. This spot must be free of both the acid you just mixed and any grease that may have accumulated on the bench.

**Above:** The author used a Smith & Wesson revolver for this project. The gun needs to be fully disassembled before bluing.

Take the firearm directly from the acid bath and rinse it thoroughly with clean running water for about 3 minutes. It often helps to bathe the piece with baking soda and water, and then rinse with water. Do not touch the metal with your hands, as that will ensure your place in history (or at least the gun's history) by leaving a print in the finish.

Still being careful not to touch the metal, swab the bluing solution onto the gun or gun part as evenly as you possibly can, and continue doing so until you can see no change in the color or darkness. In the case of a bead- or sandblasted gun, the developing color will be a good matte black. The buffed or otherwise polished gun will go through several stages of blue, black, and iridescent colors. If the color isn't fairly even, lightly acid wash it again, rinse, and reblue. It's important that the bluing goes as far as it can, or you won't get an even color or darkness. A brown color may form on the surface and this must be swabbed over with more of the solution. Remember, this is really rust that you're putting on the gun, and, therefore, you should expect to see some rust color. You must keep swabbing the brown film off so that fresh bluing solution can continue its work on the steel. After you can see no further change in the color, rinse the piece in running water and brush the brown discoloration off of its surface. I would also use a good detergent or soap to ensure that all of the discoloring rust and black particles are sloughed off with the rinse water.

Any silver solder or brass which shows after bluing can be treated at this stage with Brownells Solder Black or Birchwood Casey's Brass Black. These chemicals give the silver solder or brazing a black color that is good enough to hide the seam of either brass or silver solder. Brownells also has a soft-solder blackening agent. Rinse again after using any of these.

If air pressure is available, blow all the water off the piece and out of the threaded holes. If not, then a good water-displacing oil such as that offered by Brownells or a water-soluble oil like that used in most machine shops will work. The latter is a milky-looking emulsion after it is introduced to water. Either will work well. Oil must be used in any case. It's not good enough to just get the water off and the surfaces oiled. The firearm or part will need to be covered with an oily or greasy film for a while if it's to remain rust-free for long. You may oil the whole piece and return to it in an hour and find it bone-dry. The new surface, especially in the case of sandblasted or bead-blasted finishes, will absorb oil like you can't imagine. It still amazes me how much a matte finish will digest.

I really don't know enough theory to explain why, but it's readily apparent that the blued finish is harder after 24 hours than immediately after the process. I have found that wiping the gun with an oily rag shortly after bluing tends to leave a lot of black on the rag and thin places in the color. I have also found that leaving the real wiping off for later, say after 24 or 36 hours, will work a lot better. Reassemble the gun and let it "age" overnight or longer, and then wipe it well with a soft cloth. It may need re-oiling after the wipedown, but this should be with a cleaner oil than that which you just removed.

One way to get a real gloss without buffing is to use a stainless-steel burnishing brush on your drill press at the lowest speed available. This brush head is covered with .003-inch or finer stainless-steel wires which gently burnish the surface to a luster. XXXX-grade steel wool will do nearly as well if you have patience. It is essential that there be no moisture or shiny oil on the surfaces being burnished, or the brush or steel wool will do more than burnish the finish—it will really thin it out. This burnishing will not leave you the black-black of the matte bluing, so don't do it if you want the black to remain. The good dull black will change to a sheen of a gunmetal-gray color. I know of no reliable chemical which will give a truly glossy black without resorting to a hot process.

One last thing before you show the gun to its owner: Clean up all of the screw heads for him. Nothing ruins the looks of a newly refinished gun more than damaged screw slots. The owner may not know what's bothering him—just that something is.

I put the offending screw in a drill chuck on which I installed a handle and peen the burrs of the ruined screw slot back in place. A touch with a file, Scotchbrite wheel, or fine sandpaper before bluing the heads will do wonders. The screw heads usually don't have to go through the acid bath if they have been degreased and sanded or Scotchbrite cleaned. Buffing helps the looks of them, but will require acid before taking the bluing well. Oil and reinstall the screws, and the gun should make you proud.

I would suggest that you take before and after pictures of each gun you blue until you gain confidence. It always helps to show the owner the before and after pictures when he picks up the gun. If I know there won't be time for that, I often take a quick Polaroid shot of the gun as it was brought in so that I will have a subtle reminder to give to the owner. ★

# 20.

# Modifying a Trigger To Suit the Shooter

*The ultimate trigger job doesn't have to end with smoothing internal parts: Reshape and resurface the trigger itself.*

M
any shooters endure uncomfortable trigger shapes and surfaces—without doing anything to improve their feel or function. Nevertheless, it's relatively easy to modify a trigger to suit the individual shooter's taste.

*by Chip Todd*

We'll deal first with smoothing away serrations and sharp edges that can be uncomfortable during long shooting sessions. Then, we'll tackle widening and/or reshaping a narrow trigger to spread out the contact between finger and trigger. This can produce what feels like a lighter trigger pull. Just keep in mind that the trigger must always be slightly narrower than the width of the trigger guard, so the trigger won't hang up when holstering the gun. Steps that are common to smoothing, reshaping, and widening triggers, such as beadblasting, and bluing or plating, will be consolidated toward the end of the article.

As with any modification jobs, it's important to think through the whole process before starting any of it, to make sure you can pull it off without having to call in expensive help. Since the scope of this article is limited, and there are so many firearms that you might choose to modify, I would suggest one of the fine books from DBI or *Gun Digest* if you need assistance in disassembling and assembling the firearm.

Smoothing away serrations or sharp edges will require a small die grinder (or Dremel tool), small files, sandpaper, and some sort of surface finishing material. The grinder should have some mounted grinding stones, smoothing wheels (such as Cratex wheels), and small cotton buffing wheels or felt bobs. Hand-held abrasive sticks and sandpaper wrapped around a wooden dowel can be used in place of the die

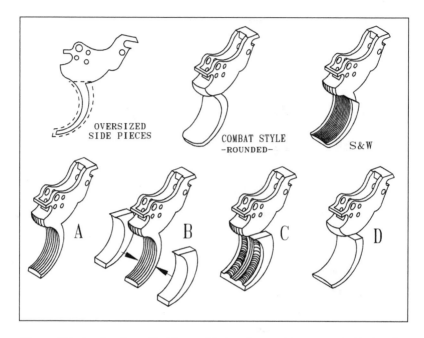

*Above:* This drawing shows the trigger-widening steps and two suggested styles of widened triggers. "A" is the normal narrow-style trigger common to revolvers. "B" shows the two side pieces to be added. "C" shows high-bead welds on face side. "D" shows a ground, square-cornered trigger before blending the edges and corners.

grinder, but be prepared to supply quite a bit of elbow grease.

The widening procedure will require the same equipment and tools used to remove the serrations, plus some sort of welding apparatus. You can probably find some metal pieces around your shop to weld to the sides of the trigger. I find it most useful to have a Scotchbrite wheel to use in deburring and smoothing or blending a surface or edge.

There are only two types of trigger surfaces offered to shooters on most factory handguns—serrated or smooth. The modified smooth surface can also be purchased on some guns with matte finishes, but most buyers are stuck with what comes on the model of gun they purchase. With the narrow triggers that come on most service handguns, the serrations have much more of an effect on the index finger than do the serrations on wider target triggers.

Have you noticed that the triggers on combat guns tend to be smooth and the triggers on target guns are often serrated? I've wondered why one would want more grip on the surface of a trigger for target-shooting than would be required in a combat situation. Am I missing something? Since shooting at targets usually goes on much longer than any urban combat situation likely would, and since my trigger finger stops appreciating the serrations after about 10 minutes of shooting, I've gotten into the habit of grinding serrations off of all my triggers. A shooters who balances his fingertip on the trigger might want lots of roughness, however.

Adding serrations to a curved surface is somewhat harder than removing them, so let's leave that to some other time. For now, let's look at removing any serrations or sharp edges that offend our sense of comfort. We can control how the finger meets the metal.

The choice of whether or not you modify a trigger could hinge on whether or not it is blued, case-colored, plated, or stainless. Obviously, the easiest to work on is the stainless-steel trigger, as it needs no finishing other than smoothing and polishing. If your gun is blued, the chances are that it will have either a blued trigger or one that has had case coloring on it. The latter finish is harder for the amateur to accomplish, but not impossible. Bluing can be done with a good cold-bluing compound and some care. Later on, I'll tell you how I deal with case-colored triggers.

Often I change the shape of a trigger to favor the hand the owner uses to shoot. This usually means that the right side of the trigger is rounded more for right-handed shooters, and the left side is rounded more for left-handers. If the person rolls his finger all the way around the trigger, both sides should be rounded somewhat. I even had one owner ask me to leave the center land of a serrated trigger so that he could feel where the center of the trigger was. This was a bit more complicated than smoothing off all of the lands and grooves.

I've found it easiest to grind serrations with my Dremel tool, as the die grinder is somewhat larger and more aggressive than the job calls for. However, I have used a die grinder with success, and I'm sure that there are a world full of people who have much steadier hands than I. The major portion of the trigger should be ground with a mounted stone; steel burrs will almost always chatter and give a rough surface. I use a stone of about 3/4-inch diameter and run the tool at about one-half speed. The easiest way I've found to keep the original shape of the trigger intact is to grind from the outside edges inward, until I have only a hint of the grooves left. This leaves the maximum amount of trigger, while still maintaining the shape. Then, changing to a finer stone, I remove the remaining grooves all the way to the top of the trigger.

This is the time to start rounding the edges until they feel good to the trigger finger. Special attention should be paid to the end of the trigger, so that there are no sharp corners left. It is quite easy for sharp corners to get enough purchase on the finger to cause pinching. That's not easy to explain away. I always try to keep the trigger's shape like the original, unless the owner and I have agreed on another shape.

Assemble the trigger back into the gun, with enough parts to allow you to try it in the gun. It might hit your finger in a different place when installed than it did when you were just holding it against your finger with the other hand.

If all feels well, disassemble and finish up the surfaces with a Cratex wheel in the Dremel. Cratex is a brand name for a polishing wheel that is made of rubber impregnated with an abrasive. I have used wheels that are impregnated with both carborundum and diamond dust, and have found that either will work well on a minor job like this. Of course, as with any process that removes something from a metal object, the trigger will become hot during the grinding or polishing, so use gloves or keep some water handy to cool the workpiece. After the Cratex, I follow with either a felt bob or a cotton polishing wheel and jeweler's rouge to achieve a mirror finish.

Even if I want the finish to be matte, I find that the sides and back look much better shiny to contrast against the matte finish. A matte finish can be accomplished with beadblasting, and will take the cold-bluing much better than polished. An alternative to matte would be a brushed finish which can be done with a fine stone and a low speed on the Dremel. Care must be taken for the scratch pattern of the stone to remain all in the same direction or it will look amateurish.

While wide triggers are not to everyone's liking, or suitable for every application, I find that most of my shooting benefits from having widened the triggers on most of my revolvers. Smith & Wesson revolvers could be purchased with wide, serrated target triggers, or semi-wide, smooth combat triggers. S&W once offered the wide triggers as an aftermarket item for guns that didn't come with wide triggers. The target triggers were even offered for installation in J-frame guns, and we all know that the small, round grips aren't suited for accuracy, so these J-frame target triggers must have been meant for revolvers like the Model 34 with a square butt.

About a decade ago, S&W discontinued selling the extra-wide triggers after some owners (rumors say policemen) jammed their loaded revolvers into their holsters and shot themselves in the leg or foot. I still prefer the wide triggers so much that I have even widened the trigger on my son's 1911 when I converted his radical .45 to a swing-trigger action. (After McCormick came out with his fine triggers at such a good price, I quit spending $300 worth of labor to do what his triggers do for a pittance.) I have never liked the looks of a trigger shoe, but I did use them before I got the right equipment to do my own trigger widening. One of the first steps needed before doing any cutting or grinding on the trigger is to determine what type of metal the trigger is made of. Some of the cheaper weapons will have die-cast triggers of a zinc or aluminum alloy. These will not lend themselves well to either smoothing or widening. Be sure that there is enough steel in the trigger to weld easily. The stainless-steel alloy that is most suited to triggers would have enough steel in it to react to a good magnet. Chrome plating will add to the difficulty of doing any smoothing or widening, as chrome doesn't weld with ordinary methods. Silver-soldering can be done over chrome, however.

I learned the hard way that it doesn't pay to use a softer metal for the side pieces, as the softer metal will erode away more than the harder steel when you're buffing the face of the trigger before plating. And be sure that the metal you are going to add to the original trigger will

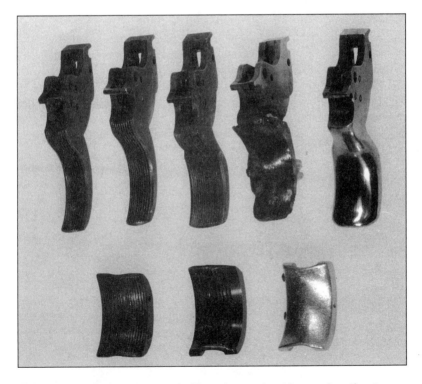

**Above:** *These Smith & Wesson double-action revolver triggers show the standard serrated trigger (bottom left), a smoothed narrow trigger (top, progression of work shown left to right), and the trigger widened and plated (bottom right).*

lend itself to the final surface treatment you have planned. Brass black will not match the bluing of steel, and some metals won't blue as well as others.

I usually choose to do the widening in the style that Smith & Wesson did when they still made the target trigger. This has rather square edges and fullness near the top of the trigger, and isn't rounded over near the sides of the trigger blade. I do this so that the trigger will look more like the older factory jobs, although I have found that rounding the edges will feel much better. It all depends on what the owner prefers. I have the trigger on my favorite S&W Model 19 shaped like a spoon; that is, rounded at the top somewhat like the portion of the spoon nearing the handle. This turned out to be the best feeling of all the shapes that I tried, although I wouldn't do this to another's gun unless he had seen my gun and another with the more conventional shape. The spoon-like trigger has thinned-out edges, while the factory trigger had edges almost 0.10 inch wide.

You'll want to decide how wide you want to go before starting on the actual modifying of the trigger. Although I usually start with pieces of metal that will be wide enough (about 1/8 inch per side), they will probably be ground back a bit narrower before the trigger is ready for the smoothing process. I set a limit of 1/2 inch wide for revolver triggers, but I won't make one any wider than the trigger guard. This has led me into widening some trigger guards for some owners, but that is usually more work than the wider trigger is worth. A 3/8-inch-wide trigger is a good compromise for most shooters.

Begin the job by holding the gun and feeling the trigger. Look at it in relation to the width of the trigger guard to see if there is room for im-

*Right:* TIG welding is ideal for adding pieces to the sides of a trigger. Notice the clamp used as a heat sink.

**Left:** *Rough grinding of the welds on the welded-up trigger can be done easily with a Dremel or similar rotary tool and a mounted stone.*

provement without the trigger becoming wider than the guard. After the proper width is decided upon, disassemble the pistol or revolver to the stage of taking the trigger out. I rough cut the metal to be added into a strip about 1/8 inch wide and long enough to cover the side of the trigger. The vise will aid in bending it to match the curve of the trigger and it should be ground to touch the sides of the trigger or a bit of fill weld will have to be done. I don't mind doing some fill welding as this insures that the weld will be fully penetrating through the trigger.

Since most triggers aren't plated, no special work need to be done to remove a surface finish. A simple magnet test will tell you if the trigger is of a non-magnetic stainless steel, although I would use stainless steel welding rod on any trigger that was "white" metal and not case-colored or blued.

Before lighting the torch to weld on the trigger, I clamp the trigger to a heat sinking source, being sure that the sear and nose are in contact with the heat sink. It is quite disturbing to go to all of the work of widening the trigger only to have it last just a short while. Using another clamp to hold the metal to the sides of the trigger, I weld the new metal all along the interface between them and the trigger. Don't be afraid to put on too much weld, as it is better than having to re-heat the trigger and take another chance on ruining the temper. I've actually immersed the important parts of the trigger in water while welding on other parts of the trigger. You can't cool the parts too much, but you sure can heat them too much.

After the trigger is welded, grind the curve back into the face of the trigger. I've used a Dremel tool with grinding stones, an air grinder with rotary burrs, and even a body grinder with nine-inch wheels to get the curve back into the front of the trigger. In most cases, the rear of the trigger is ground flat across and follows the curve of the face, with the trigger getting thicker toward the top. It should be easy to follow the original shape of the backside.

At this point, I usually go to the disk sander to flatten out the sides, although a hand file would suffice. After the width of the trigger is

*Right:* Nickel plating of the trigger can be done with the Texas Platers Supply plating rig. A copper base is used to seal the steel off and to aid in the nickel plating. It's surprising how well such a simple kit works.

reached, and the additions on each side are symmetrical, the decision on whether or not to accommodate lefties must be made. Since I have other guns for left-handed friends to shoot, I make the triggers on my personal favorites more comfortable for my right-hand shooting. This means that I round the edges off more on the right side of the trigger, and make sure that the upper part of the right-hand side of the trigger doesn't bite into the top of my index finger. I don't recommend this for everybody; you must decide this for yourself.

The face of the trigger should have a crown to it so that the finger won't feel pressure on the outside edges of the surface. I usually strive for about a 4-inch radius, although this is another thing that you can feel as you grind. This final shaping is easily done with a Dremel tool and a 1/2-inch sanding drum, or it can be done with mounted stones. I find that I can get a better surface with the drum than I can with a stone. The grinding is followed by either a Cratex wheel or some sandpaper around your finger. If you can see any pits or occlusions in the surface of the welded areas, it may be necessary to re-weld those areas to get a good solid surface.

I put the semi-finished trigger back into the gun and try it for feel before going any further. This might also be a good time to try it in a holster, to see if the trigger can drag on the sides while holstering the gun. It may be that you will have to take some more of the width off to insure that it won't leave the owner with nine toes.

If it passes this holster test, check out the shape again, and then do the finish buffing and polishing. Again, Cratex, Scotchbrite, and a cloth wheel with rouge will help bring the finish up to a shine. Triggers were meant to be noticed. If you feel otherwise, the surface can be dulled to a matte finish using glassbeading or sandblasting with fine silica.

If you buffed the finish, the wax from the rouge must be removed before bluing or plating. When I need to remove the wax and grease from such metal, I usually use deodorized kerosene, some trichloroethane 1,1,1, and acetone. This is usually enough to allow a good bluing or plating. I do the plating of small parts with the Texas Plating Kit which gives quite a good, hard plating, except for gold plating which is soft. Even the gold lasts for several years on most guns. Their nickel plating in the kit is just as good as any factory finish, and can be selectively plated on certain areas. I use it on all the contacting surfaces inside the gun that I can, as nickel has a lower coefficient of friction than steel.

If you've chosen bluing, there are three common choices of surfaces—matte, brushed, and polished. The matte finish is the easiest cold bluing to use, and gives a very dull black finish. I use Brownells Oxpho-Blue, as I've had better luck with it than any other I've tried. Brownells Dicropan IM is also another good one that many gunsmiths swear by.

To begin the process, clean the metal with solvent, and apply the cold bluing compound with a swab, rag, or tissue. Follow this with a water rinse and some water-displacing oil and let the oil soak in. Polished or brushed surfaces are somewhat harder to get free of grease or wax, but persistence will pay off in less aggravation in applying the bluing.

Case coloring the trigger—or any other part for that matter—is not as easy as you might think. I send all of my case-coloring jobs to Ben Wood of Buena Park, California, who's just about the best bluer I have ever run across. He gives quick turn-around and I have always gotten world-class bluing from him. His case coloring is quite close to the old coloring found on pristine collector firearms.

After doing the bluing or plating of the trigger, only the final reassembly remains. This must be done with careful attention to cleanliness, to avoid introducing any grit that can wear the action. I use deodorized kerosene in my cleaning tanks, as it doesn't evaporate very rapidly and isn't harsh on the hands. While it is combustible, it isn't as dangerous as gasoline or naphtha. And the smell doesn't pervade the entire shop.

After closing up the gun, try the trigger for feel. I think you'll be proud of yourself for producing a gun that's much more pleasing to shoot. It should be easy to feel the change. ★

# 21.

# How to Sharpen a Tungsten-Carbide Drill

*Using an oil stone and a homemade jig, you can sharpen an ordinary masonry bit enough to cut almost any hard metal.*

*by Walt Netzel*

Th=hey will drill case-hardened steel, saws, drills, broken taps, easy outs, tempered tool steel, even files. These drills are available in most hardware stores, starting at 1/8 inch and increasing in diameter in 1/16-inch increments. Expect to pay about $2 depending on the size. But they're sold to drill masonry; they aren't sharp enough to cut metal as they come from the package. There are several ways to sharpen them. An ordinary silicon-carbide wheel won't do the job, not because it isn't hard enough but because the worn grains of abrasive won't flake off the wheel. A diamond wheel is the best tool for this job, but they cost about $100 and are easily damaged. A less expensive choice is a green silicon carbide wheel, costing about $30. This is a soft wheel and it will wear rapidly. A green cloud of dust comes off when you use it, and it doesn't do as good a job as a diamond wheel. Both wheels will get the drill hot—but don't cool it in water; it's likely to crack.

A good, inexpensive, but slower method uses an ordinary silicon carbide oil stone. This method requires a jig to hold the drill at the proper angle. You can easily make one from a short length of 2x4 and a short length of a large dowel. With this type of drill, the clearance angle is 24 degrees rather than the 12 degrees of a twist drill. Also note that the lip angle is 64 degrees rather than 59 degrees.

To make a drill-sharpening jig, start with an 18-inch length of 2x4. Set your table saw blade to 64 degrees from horizontal, and rip a long wedge from one side, leaving the remaining wood 3 1/2 inches wide at the widest side. Without changing the angle of the blade, cut a kerf or slot 1 inch in from the beveled edge (parallel to it) and 12 inches

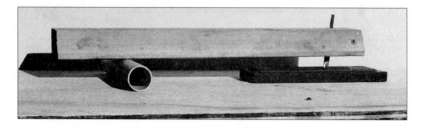

**Above:** *The wooden jig holds the drill at precisely the right angle; you need only to roll it back and forth over the stone.*

long. Drill a clearance hole in the 1-inch resulting projection, about an inch from the end, for a 2-inch flathead wood screw. Insert a screw and tighten it enough to prevent the projection from flexing away from the body of the 2x4, but not tight enough to close the kerf.

The next step is to drill a series of holes in the slot. Use a scrap of plywood about 8 by 12 inches to hold the 2x4 at the proper angle while drilling. Draw a line through the lower corner, 24 degrees up from the long side, and nail the narrow beveled edge of the 2x4 (bottom of the 1-inch projection) to the line. Use small wire nails for this temporary joint. Nail the end of the 1-inch wide projection exactly 3 1/8 inches back along the line from the corner. If all has been done correctly, the plywood scrap should stand vertically; if it doesn't, shim or trim the lower corner of the 2x4 until the plywood does stand vertically. This holds the 2x4 at the correct angle for drilling vertical holes through the center of the kerf.

Drill a vertical body-sized hole through the kerf for each size drill you

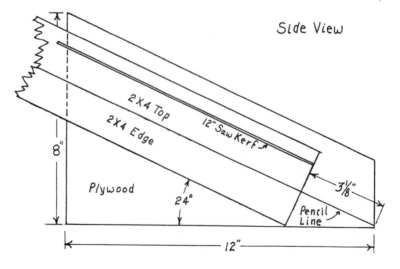

will want to sharpen. Remember, the bodies of these drills are smaller than the cutting tips. The first hole should be about 3/4 inch behind the wood screw, and leave at least the same amount of space between the rest of the holes. Use a drill press if you have one. This will ensure that the holes are vertical. Pull the plywood off the 2x4 after the holes are drilled.

To use the jig, insert a drill in the appropriate hole. Turn the cutting edge so it's at a right angle to the length of the 2x4, and clamp it lightly in place with the wood screw. Place the roller (the short dowel) under the rear end of the jig and an oil stone under the tip of the drill at the other end. Adjust the depth of the drill in its hole to level the jig, then tighten the clamping wood screw to hold the drill in place.

Oil your stone and make just two passes with the drill. Then turn the jig over and look at the bit. The fresh grind mark should be in the center of the flat face. If it isn't, adjust the lip angle by rotating the drill in its hole slightly, and adjust the cutting angle by changing the depth of the drill slightly. This will ensure that the drill is sharpened to its original angles. If you don't exactly match these angles, the drill will still cut equally well, but you will have to remove more metal than is necessary, with more wear on your oil stone.

If you're not careful, you can wear a rut in your oil stone. Avoid this by using a circular motion, distributing the wear over the entire stone. Use only a light pressure; these drills will wear your stone a lot faster than tool steel.

When you have removed about half of the necessary metal from the cutting face, rotate the drill 180 degrees and grind the other face. By alternating between faces and cutting only small increments, it will be easier to keep the lips equal in length.

Keep in mind that this method will eventually sharpen your drill *too* sharp. The granular nature of tungsten carbide can't support the fine edge an oil stone produces, so a little of the cutting edge will flake away in use. To prevent this flaking, remove the drill from the jig and

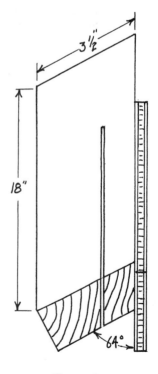

End View

make one pass with a fine slip stone at a right angle to each cutting edge. While this will imperceptibly "dull" the drill, it will greatly prolong the life of the cutting edge.

Test your sharpening job on a piece of glass. I use an old shot glass with a little water in it. If your drill will cut glass, it will cut all the different metals you might want to use it on. ★

# 22.

# Modifying .22 Tubular Magazines

*You can't possibly stock every rimfire tube magazine you'll ever need—unless you learn how to build your own.*

*By Jim Thompson*

One of the most problematic pieces on .22 rimfire repeating rifles that have magazine tubes are the tubes themselves. You will often see tubes that have been turned the wrong way and damaged, and you will want to fix the tubes.

The gunsmith's problem is from a stocking situation; you'll go broke stocking all the many varieties of magazine tubes offered by manufacturers. A better, cheaper option is to stock only the longest tubes—I generally prefer Remington tubes because I get a break on them—and then cut them down to fit.

You can usually fashion a magazine tube to fit a gun as long as the tube you are using is longer than the one you need—almost all .22 rimfire magazine tubes are the same diameter. There are a few exceptions, however, which makes checking them worth the trouble, but in general, you can modify a few magazine tubes to fit many different rifles.

Here are two ways to perform this job.

## Method One

If the distance from the pin that holds the gun's magazine tube into the outer magazine tube is the same as your replacement tube, proceed as follows:

● Insert the inside magazine tube into the outside magazine tube until the follower touches the carrier. Do not compress the follower; you want it to just touch the carrier. If it is compressed against the carrier, it will protrude and lock up the action on the last shot.

● When you are satisfied that the inside magazine tube is positioned

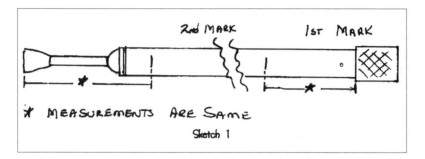

2nd MARK    1st MARK

✻ MEASUREMENTS ARE SAME

Sketch 1

correctly, mark it with an indelible pen at the top edge of the outside magazine tube.

● Remove the inside magazine tube, measure the distance from the mark to the bottom edge of the inside magazine tube's knurled head. Transfer this distance to the other end of the inside magazine tube. The distance should be measured from the end of the follower back toward the head.

● Put the inside magazine tube that you marked in the lathe with the marked end (follower end) protruding out of the lathe chuck about an inch past your mark. Put the radiused welding rod (see Tool Chest sidebar) in the drill chuck and push it in, compressing the magazine follower until it is past the point where your mark is. With a V-shaped cutter or a cutoff tool, cut through the inside magazine tube at your mark. The rod will hold the follower in. After you have cut through the tube slide, put the cutoff piece back against the drill chuck and square off the cut.

● Measure the distance from the end of the tube to the indent that holds the follower in on the cut off piece. You will want to make your indent the same distance from the new end. With your tubing cutter gradually increase the tension on the cutter until you have an indent that will hold the follower in. Use the cut off end as a guide.

● Next, put the modified center drill in the drill chuck and use it to push the follower into the inside magazine tube. Continue in with the center drill until it reams the inside end of the inside magazine tube.

● Install the inside magazine tube into the gun test fire it.

## Method Two

If the distance between the replacement hold-in pin and the head on the tube is different from the gun's tube, slight adjustments can be made by turning the bottom end of the head the same diameter as the magazine tube to increase the distance between the hold in pin and the bottom of the head. Otherwise, proceed as follows:

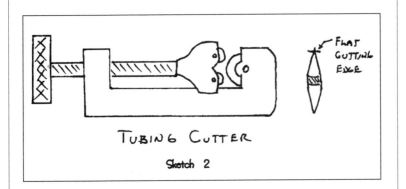

TUBING CUTTER

Sketch 2

# Tool Chest

To work on magazine tubes, I use three tools I have made or modified.

● Modified tubing cutter. This is a standard item available in any hardware store, except I modify the cutting wheel. Flatten the cutting edge until it is about $^1/_{16}$ inch across and round the edges slightly. (Also, this item can be purchased from Brownells already made up.)

● A piece of $^1/_4$-inch welding rod about 6 inches long, with one end radiused.

● A center drill (the size isn't important, as long as the diameter is larger than the inside of the magazine tube. I use an old $^1/_2$-inch one.) Flatten the point on one end so it will not cut.

● Remove the head of the inside magazine tube. Insert the inside magazine tube into the gun and mark as previously explained. This time you will also need to mark the point where the retaining pin will be reinstalled. Use the outside magazine tube as a guide and mark it with a fine-point indelible pen.

● Drive out the retaining pin. Holding the tube while you do this can be a problem, but I made a bench block with a groove cut across the top to hold the tube and then made a hole near the edge to receive the pin as it is driven out. Most bench blocks don't have a hole close enough to the edge to accommodate this. Cut the inside magazine tube at your mark. To maintain the same tension on the magazine follower, cut the magazine spring by the length of the cut off.

● Reinstall the head, turning the hole in the shank 180 degrees from the hole you are going to drill. If you clamp the tube in a drill vise, it will hold the head in while you are drilling. Use a center drill to start the hole and drill completely through the tube and head with a bit that will give you a friction fit on the pin.

● With the tube still in the vise, drive the pin in until it protrudes just beyond the opposite side. Remove and grind the pin flush with the tube. A belt sander is best for this.

To finish up, you install the tube in the gun and test-fire it. You've successfully made a simple replacement item that will save you time, money and stockroom work—and make your repeating .22s feed rimfire ammunition smoothly.                                    ★

# 23.

# Pillar Bedding: A Metal Route To Better Accuracy

*Inserting aluminum rods through a rifle stock stabilizes the action better than wood ever could.*

*By AG Staff*

Many of the accuracy advantages sport hunters enjoy today were first pursued and perfected by benchrest shooters. This cadre of shooting perfectionists continually works to squeeze that last thousandth of an inch off group sizes. Using fiberglass as a bedding material is one development transferred from benchrest shooting to hunting rifles, and now another benchrest innovation—adding pillar bedding to a glassed-in action job—seems to be catching on.

Even though glass bedding takes up all of the inletting error between wood and metal, it doesn't do much to prevent the underlying wood fibers from collapsing over time. During the time wood leaves the tree trunk and becomes a gun stock, it dries, which leaves all the tiny wood capillaries that once fed the tree empty. Tightening action screws and the shock of the gun firing will collapse the capillaries over time and eventually cause the bedding to go sour.

However, this compression process can be arrested by adding sleeves around the action screws when you perform a glass-bedding job. The sleeves act as braces between the barreled action and the bottom metal, preventing any compression of the wood fibers beneath the epoxy bedding.

## Making Pillars

The two most commonly used materials to make these pillars are aluminum and nylon, so there is no danger of rust. Over the years I've used both aluminum and nylon to make action screw sleeves, and I can't say that one works better than the other. For the most part I start out with half-inch-diameter aluminum or nylon rod and then turn it down in the lathe to 0.490 inches. I'll explain why later. The exposed end is then faced off square and a starting hole is center drilled into the end of the rod. I normally turn two or three grooves, 0.030 inch deep, into the outside of the sleeve with an 0.125-inch-wide groove tool. The center-drilled starter hole is then drilled to a depth of one inch with an I drill. I chamfer the hole slightly and also the outside edge of the sleeve.

Then, cut off the sleeve from the rod to a length of 1 inch. The cut off end is faced off square and chamfered at the hole and the outside edge. Two of these sleeves are required for most bolt-action rifles. In the case of the Winchester Model 70 where there are three screws, only the front action screw and the rear trigger guard screw require a pillar. The front trigger guard screw does not need one. I use a "letter I" drill (0.277 inches) to drill the center hole because most bolt-action rifles use two $1/4$-inch-diameter action screws with threads from 22 to 34 per inch. The extra 0.027 inches in size gives enough clearance to prevent any interference in fit. When I make up these sleeves, I usually make several extra so some are handy for hurry-up jobs.

The action-screw holes in the stock will now need to be drilled out so that these two sleeves can go in. This step is tricky and should be done in a drill press. Clamp the stock in your drillpress vise making sure there is some provision to protect the stock from the vise jaws. Using a small machinist level, level the stock in the vise with the action inletting up. Chuck a 0.500-inch drill in the drill chuck and drill out the rear action-screw hole. but only about half way through. The same is done for the front action-screw hole in the stock. Invert the stock in the vise, but this time level the trigger guard and floorplate inletting. Drill out the action-screw holes until they meet the hole that was drilled from the other side. By doing it this way there is less chance of a crooked hole being drilled into the stock. Turning the sleeves down to 0.490 inch allows them to fit into the 0.500-inch drilled hole with some clearance. If the sleeve diameter and the hole are both 0.500 inch in diameter, you run the risk of splitting the stock in this area when forcing the sleeve down into place. Check the sleeves to see that they will slip into the two drilled holes without any excessive resistance and polish with No. 220 grit emery paper if they seem to go in hard.

## Installation

I use Brownells Acra-Weld to epoxy these sleeves in place. The grooves are turned into the sides of these sleeves so I can fill them with epoxy and prevent any upward or downward movement of the sleeves once the epoxy sets. Mix up whatever epoxy you prefer and coat the

**Right:** *A liquid floor wax—if you can find one—works well as a release agent for epoxy bedding compounds. A paste wax also works well, and can be made easier to use by dissolving in a little naphtha.*

outside of the sleeves and poke some into the two drilled holes. Coat the inside hole of the pillar sleeve for the action screws with release agent in case any epoxy gets in there. I normally place the bottom metal back into the stock to prevent gravity from allowing the sleeves to move and clamp the bottom metal lightly in place with a woodworkers clamp. Make sure to put release agent on the bottom metal so that it doesn't get glued in place. After the epoxy cures, clean up any excess around the sleeves at the bottom of the stock inletting. The top of the sleeves can be dressed down to the inletting with a carbide burr bit in your Moto-tool if the inletting is for a round-bottomed receiver like those used by Remington. If you are dealing with a flat-bottomed receiver such as those on the Mauser 98 or Winchester Model 70, a piloted counter-bore tool can be used to dress the top of each sleeve down until it is flush with the surrounding wood.

There are some instances where the outside diameter of the sleeve to be used needs to be smaller than what was described here. One rifle where this comes into play is the 600 series Remingtons that use a #10-

32 rear action screw. Here of course a smaller diameter sleeve would be better or in any instance where the outside diameter of the pillar would not be hidden by the action tang. As long as there is enough wall thickness on the pillar to support the action, adjusting the outside diameter is no problem. Here I would use a 0.375 inch diameter rod turned down to 0.365 inch and then drill the stock holes with a 0.375 inch drill bit in the same manner as described earlier. The diameter of the #10-32 screw is about 0.187 inch, so a number 4 drill bit would give a 0.207 inch diameter through hole in the pillar.

In the event you are not able to make your own action sleeves for pillar bedding, Brownells has some available that are very similar to those described here.

## A Note About Release Agents

More years ago than I care to remember, I became disenchanted with the high price of commercial release agents for use with glass-bedding compounds. I felt that there must be a cheaper alternative. After a bit of research, I discovered that the fiberglass industry has used wax sold for wood floors as a release agent for their molds—and has been using it for years. The key ingredient is carnauba wax.

Armed with this information, I purchased a container of Johnson's Beauti-Flor wax and tried it on the next glass bedding job I did. I was very pleased with the results. It was as effective as any release agent I had tried, regardless of price.

I use it in the following manner: Prepare the stock in the usual manner. Clean the action and anywhere the glass (epoxy) will contact the rifle. Use modeling clay to fill in any voids that would tend to lock up in the bedding. Put masking tape on the front of the recoil lug. This facilitates the removal of the barreled action from the stock. Using a small paint brush, paint the wax on all areas that will contact the glass bedding, giving special attention to stock screw holes and stock screws. When completely painted, I then blow off the excess with compressed air. This assures that the wax gets into every crevice and also speeds up drying of the wax. From here on it's just like any other bedding job.

I finally used up the original container that had lasted me about 20 years and tried to buy some more. Much to my surprise, I could not find it in any of the local stores. I called S.C. Johnson & Sons, and was told that it was no longer being manufactured, and that they were not making any replacement for it. It seems that the floor-covering industry has changed over the years, and the demand for the wax is no longer there. The person I talked to was not very knowledgeable about the product, and could or would not give me any help.

I was able to find S.C. Johnson Paste Wax for wood floors. I purchased a can and, on examination, it appeared to be the same material in a paste form. I experimented with reducing it to a liquid, and found that naphtha (lighter fluid) could be used as a reducing agent. Reduce the paste until it is the consistency of heavy cream, and store in an airtight container. The ingredients are no longer listed on the container, but the active ingredient that makes it work is carnauba wax. I could find very little information on carnauba wax other than it is a vegetable product that comes from the leaves of the carnauba palm tree.

In any event, it works, and it's less expensive than commercial release agents. ★

# 24.

## The Ins and Outs of Making Springs

*Making your own springs can solve a variety of problems—if it is done correctly. Here are the basics.*

*by Frank Fry*

In talking with a gunsmith colleague the other day, we came to the conclusion that the art of flat-spring making seems to be dying. He was bemoaning the fact that he couldn't find a V-spring for a shotgun. He complained that he had to buy a complete set from Brownells just to find the one that came closest. And even then it didn't fit...and it was too expensive...and on and on.

Why not make one? He had made dozens of others, but somehow they never worked. He had the wrong steel...they were too soft...too brittle...he didn't have a furnace with a sensitive enough heat control.... His problem was easy to see. Not realizing how simple and easy spring making is, he had set immovable obstacles in his path.

As a practical spring maker in a practical setting, a knowledge of the molecular changes that take place in steel during heat treating is not really necessary. Much akin to driving a car, it's not necessary to know how the valves open and close in order to start the engine. The important thing is: "Will it start when I turn the key?"

There are two general types of springs used in gun work—the wound or "coil spring" and the flat spring.

The coil spring is found behind extractors, firing pins, and some hammers. Very little breakage occurs with these springs, and inexpensive spring kits are available in great profusion to fit this need. The easiest way to handle a broken coil spring is to find the closest replacement from the kit and trim it to fit. This is not true when trying to replace a flat spring.

The flat spring is divided into two general categories: the single-leaf flat spring and the V-spring. The flat spring can be used in combination

***Above:*** *Old clock or automobile springs make good starting points for building springs for firearms.*

with active parts like the trigger/bolt spring in single-action operation. It may also be incorporated as an integral part of another unit such as the Luger ejector. Some of these flat springs may be simply roughed out, while others may require the careful fitting of many dimensions.

The double-leaf or V-spring is associated with many high-grade doubles and over/unders. The top-lever return spring on many less expensive break-open shotguns can also be a spring of this type. The double-leaf spring is used as a hammer spring in many side-lock actions, both of modern and black-powder vintage. These springs vary from a simple bend in a general U-shape, to those requiring integral retaining pins, intricate stirrup loops, and careful load balancing of each leg of the spring.

Since the coil spring (which is actually a spiral spring) causes little trouble and is easily replaced from a spring kit, it is the flat spring that gives us the most trouble. The process of making a flat spring consists of several basic and simple steps, and any shop that has an oxyacetylene torch, a vise, a few files, and a gunsmith worthy of the name is equipped to do the job.

For ease in understanding the process, the steps are broken down into several categories. Let's look at each one of these points from a practical standpoint; in other words, spring making made easy and profitable:

## Spring-Stock Selection

Steel is selected to fit the spring shape and size. Our favorite suppliers stock a number of flat-spring kits. A number of these kits can be ordered and kept on hand to fill all possible needs, but a great deal of money can be tied up in stock. Fortunately, alternative sources for inexpensive spring steel may be found in unlikely places.

One not so unlikely source is the local watchmaker. A visit to the clock-repair shop will often yield clock springs that have been broken—useless for clocks, ideal for firearms. Sometimes all that's needed is to voice an interest in the broken springs, and the repair shop will be happy to give them to you to clean out the junk drawer. Heavy clock springs make excellent top-lever springs for Iver Johnson single-shot shotguns. Smaller clock springs can be used for single-action trigger/bolt or hand springs, and other applications where a lighter-weight spring is required.

Clock springs are not suitable for hammer springs or other applications requiring thicker stock. These springs can be fashioned out of flat automobile springs. Visit your friendly junk-car emporium and purchase a couple of spring leaves from cars made through the early 40s. The steel in these is excellent for gun springs. More modern automobile springs are filled with exotic alloys that may make great car springs, but the heat-treating is vastly different, and they're not suitable for our purposes.

## Annealing

Annealing is the term for removing the temper from steel to make it soft and workable. Both clock and car springs are tempered as springs, and will have to be annealed before use.

The process of annealing steel is to heat it to just above the point where the steel loses its magnetic qualities. This is to a dull or medium red, or about 1200 degrees. Several methods can be used to anneal, all giving good results.

When first using a clock or automobile spring, I suggest you make a "test" spring to verify that the steel will do what you want it to do. The directions will be the same for making a replacement spring. Hacksaw off and polish a manageable-size piece of spring stock.

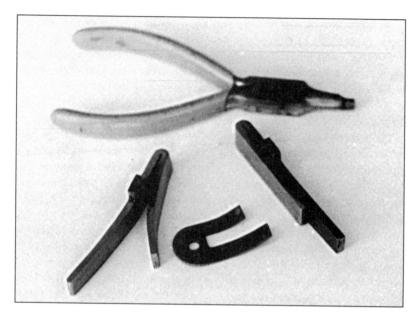

*Above: Clock and car springs can quickly and easily be turned into finished firearms springs like those shown in the foreground.*

For the average shop, this annealing method works well: Apply heat to the spring blank until "colors" appear. These colors should pass from yellow through blue, then to a dull gray, and finally to dull or medium red. At this point, remove the heat and let the stock cool slowly to room temperature. The spring section should now be annealed and soft enough to work. This method will work on most spring stock, and is the easiest method to use in small-shop applications.

Test the annealed part with a file. It should cut easily. When dropped on an anvil, the part should sound leaden or dull. It should also stay put when bent. If it does not cut easily; if it rings or resists bending; re-anneal with increased heat.

At this point, the test section should be hardened and drawn to make sure the steel becomes a spring. Needless to say, if you finish a spring without this test, any error will always be on the brittle side, and the spring will break. Conduct a thorough test of hardening and drawing processes before laying out and shaping. These tests will be discussed in more detail later on in this article.

## Making the Pattern

If the broken parts of the spring are available, lay out the design of the spring by gluing or soldering the original parts to the annealed spring section for scribing. Or if that's impractical, use layout dye and transfer the dimensions to the spring blank. This method works well when mirror-imaging a spring from an opposite lock. Sometimes the trial-and-error method is needed to find the shape and thickness of the original spring configuration, especially when the original spring has been lost.

A double-leaf or V-spring will have to be laid out full length, and then bent or folded to shape (leaving some extra on each end of the legs to compensate for the bend). If a retaining pin or stud is incorporated into the spring, the overall width must include the length of the pin. In this case, the excess width around the pin may be removed either before or after the spring is bent. Removal after bending can give a more accurate pin location, but requires greater care in removing excess material from the opposing leg.

## Cutting and Filing

In making a double-leaf spring, polish the inner side of the spring before bending to prevent stress points after the spring is bent. Dings, file marks, and other imperfections in the steel surface must be removed to prevent weakening the spring. Bending the spring is best done at medium-red heat. Some spring makers advocate the use of a small wire in the crease formed by the bend to produce a radius at that point. This helps to prevent the development of a breakage point.

After the newly bent spring has cooled to room temperature, cut and file the spring to shape. The legs should be tapered and thinned as required before spreading. After tapering and thinning, spread the legs to the desired radius. Shaping and bending may be done either at room temperature or at a dull-red heat. Great care should be taken to prevent angular bends in the legs and to preserve smooth curves.

If the new spring is placed in position in the firearm to check it for fit, remember that the leg opening may be altered during this fitting and additional adjustments may be required.

## Polishing

Remove any file or heavy emery marks on the outside and sides of the spring, polishing it to a full luster. Breakage can occur along file and rough emery marks the same way scoring a sheet of glass allows it to be broken. Also remove any wire edges from the finished spring.

## Set Allowance

A flat or V-spring loses some leg opening or bend during testing, and if a "set allowance" is not made, this normal change can make the new

**Right:** *Flat, folded, and spread springs are the kinds you'll deal with most.*

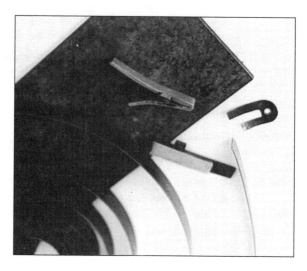

spring useless. Approximately 10 percent in extra leg opening or bend is needed to compensate for this collapse during testing. From a trial-and-error process, you'll soon discover how much compensation is needed in your spring-making applications.

## Hardening

After the spring has been satisfactorily shaped and polished, it needs to be hardened. Hardening is accomplished by heating the steel above its critical temperature (to a medium red), then cooling quickly or quenching to freeze the grain structure. The spring blank is now in a hardened state. It is also very brittle and can shatter if dropped on a concrete floor.

The quenching process for spring steels is generally done in either oil, water, or brine. Air-hardening steels are available, but the spring sections we buy in tubes, beg from the watch repairman, or get at the junk yard, most often should be hardened in oil or water. If in doubt, try the test section in oil first. If it doesn't harden, try water, then brine.

Heat the shaped spring to a bright red and hold it at that temperature to give the heat a chance to penetrate fully. An oxyacetylene torch must be used with care to keep the spring heated evenly. The spring is now plunged into oil, water, or brine and agitated rapidly to cool it as quickly as possible. Test it for hardness with a stroke or two of a file (on a noncritical edge of the spring) to make sure it has hardened. The spring should be glass hard at this point.

Note: Using water to harden an oil-hardening spring will make it hard but too brittle after drawing or tempering to be useful.

## Drawing or Tempering

This is the process which gives the spring its desirable qualities as a spring. Too hard and the spring will break; too soft and it will not return to shape. Several methods of drawing are generally accepted.

The color-change method starts with polishing the spring to remove scale and discoloration from hardening. Place the polished spring on a larger piece of steel. Heat this larger piece until the spring colors change to a medium blue. Remove the spring from the secondary heat source and allow it to cool slowly. This method requires both a fine touch with the torch and an instinct to know when to remove the spring from the heat.

Flashing is another method of tempering. Dip the spring in used motor oil and heat the spring gently with a torch until the heat of the spring sustains the burning of the oil. The burning temperature of oil is an almost exact match to the spring-drawing temperature. More oil is applied by very quickly dipping the spring in the oil. Thin springs cool quickly and may require additional heat after dipping to burn the oil. This method works well with thin, light springs which do not need a great deal of "soaking" to get heat penetration. About four or five flashings should do.

An outgrowth of flashing, known as the dip-and-heat method, is useful for slightly heavier springs. Place the hardened spring in a metal container and cover it with oil. Heat the container until the oil burns by its own heat. Let the oil burn out and allow the spring to cool. This method has one drawback: It's messy. Oil burning in the container sends a great deal of oily smoke and lots of black soot into the air. This method is best used outdoors.

The final method, which produces superior results on almost all springs, involves a hot lead bath. As lead fumes are not good for mind or body, this process is also best done outside or in a very well-ventilated area. Start by melting lead in a melting pot with a torch or other heat source. After the lead has melted, wire the hardened spring just below the surface of the lead so it does not touch either the bottom or sides of the pot. Fear not, lead will not stick to the spring, and any lead that is trapped in crevices or bends will shake off or be peeled off easily with a scriber when the spring has cooled. (Lead does not adhere like solder.) Sprinkle a few drops of oil on the top of the melted lead. Heat the pot, letting the flame play over the sides and bottom to evenly distribute the heat. As the oil smokes and dissipates, add more. Presently, the oil will begin to burn. Remove the heat and add a few more drops of oil. If the oil burns from the heat of the lead, the lead is at spring-drawing temperature, and everything suspended in it is at that temperature as well. No more heat is required. Remove the spring from the lead and allow both the spring and lead to cool to room temperature. Remember that the lead will take a long time to cool—don't try to hurry it.

## Testing

We need to see that the spring has indeed become what we need. The first test is to drop the spring on an anvil or the floor, and listen for a characteristic "ring." A soft or annealed spring will sound dull like a sandwich zinc quarter, while a hardened and drawn spring will sound like a silver quarter. If the spring rings, the next test will be to try it in a vise. Use smooth jaws to prevent marking the spring. For a single-leaf spring such as a single-action trigger/bolt or hand spring, flatten it gently and release slowly—a very easy operation. If the spring is a double-leaf or V-spring, test it by slowly bringing the arms of the spring together between the vise jaws, and then slowly releasing them. Fast compression and release can stress a new V-spring so greatly it may snap. Check the tested spring for "set" against finished dimensions which exclude your 10-percent extra for set. The tested spring should measure quite closely. After the initial squeeze test, there should be no further change after subsequent compressions. If the spread has closed too much, anneal, reshape with more spread, harden, and draw again.  ★

# 25.

# Learning Gunsmithing In the Classroom

*There are many schools that provide gunsmith training. Any of them would be a good place to hone your skills.*

*by Dan Baldwin*

Formal training is available in many localities for those wanting to enter the gunsmithing profession as a full-time occupation. Some schools are privately owned and teach gun-related courses only. Others combine these subjects with general-education college courses leading to a two-year Associate degree. The purpose of this article is to identify these institutions and provide the reader with an approximation of time requirements. The typical gunsmithing program at these schools include instruction in the following areas:

- Basic Shop
- Machine Shop
- Welding
- Metalsmithing
- Bluing and Metal Finishes
- Stock Making
- Ballistics and Handloading
- Firearms Repair
- Shop and Business Operation

The privately owned institutions usually describe their courses and program by the actual number of classroom hours; i.e., if you attend school for eight hours a day, five days a week, this is 40 hours of instruction. Most state-run colleges, on the other hand, present their educational programs in terms of units or credits. One credit is normally equal to one hour of lessons per week for the semester.

Thus, if you have a class that meets for one hour twice a week during a 13-week semester, this would be 2 credits, or 26 instructional hours (2 hours/week x 13 weeks/semester).

For ease of comparison, I have included the approximate number of actual instructional hours for those institutions that use the credit or unit system. However, fees vary, with most state-owned institutions providing substantial discounts to in-state residents. Costs include tuition, housing or living expenses, tools, supplies, and books. Completing a formal gunsmithing program will require from one to two years of attendance. Be sure to contact the institution for up-to-date price listings.

Hands-on instruction is expensive, and both time and money are necessary to accomplish a formal schooling in gunsmithing. However, financial aid of one type or another is available through all of these institutions. Thus, if the time can be found, monetary help is often possible. Many schools offer federal and state grants, and all are covered by various veterans' programs. The schools will provide information concerning the availability of financial aid and assist the potential student in preparing the applications necessary to receive these benefits. For those who can't or don't want to attend a full-time training program, each year some of these listed facilities offer NRA-sponsored "short-term gunsmithing schools" ranging from one day to two weeks in length. Cost is usually modest. These courses cover such diverse subjects as general gunsmithing to specialized instructions on the repair of one particular model gun. Additional information concerning these programs can be obtained by contacting the listed schools directly, or by calling the NRA's Gunsmithing Coordinator.

Presented in the paragraphs that follow is a listing, alphabetized by state, of all the schools I know of that offer classroom training in various gunsmithing-related studies:

## Arizona

**Yavapai College.** (1100 E. Sheldon St., Prescott, AZ 86301.) Located in central Arizona, Prescott is approximately 90 miles north of Phoenix. The 100-acre campus, situated on the grounds of old Fort Whipple where Teddy Roosevelt's Rough Riders trained, offers on-campus living. The school operates on a two-semester year and grants an Associate degree in gunsmithing. The curriculum consists of 50 credits (750 hours) in gunsmithing, plus 20 credits (300 hours) of educational classes—70 credits total (1,050 hours), requiring four semesters or two years of study.

## California

**Lassen College.** (Hwy. 139, P.O. Box 3000, Susanville, CA 96130.)

Susanville is situated in the Sierra Nevada range of northeastern California, 90 miles northwest of Reno, Nevada. The campus is large, about 165 acres, and furnishes on-campus housing. The school operates on a two-semester year, and offers both Associate degree and certificate programs. The degree program consists of 42 units (630 hours) of gunsmith courses and 18 units (270 hours) of general-educational courses—60 units (900 hours) total, requiring four semesters or two years of study. Lassen offers one-year certificate programs in the following areas: Custom Metalsmithing, 24 units (360 hours); Barrel Fitting, 16 units (240 hours); Machining for Gunsmiths, 22 units (330 hours); and Stockmaking, 17 units (255 hours). Also available at this institution after completion of the degree program is a one-year postgraduate course of 24 additional units (360 hours) of specialized gunsmithing instruction.

## Colorado

**Colorado Gunsmithing Academy of Lamar.** (27533 U. S. Hwy. 287 South, Lamar, CO 81052.) The school is in southeastern Colorado, and consists of a 15,000-square-foot building, gun-repair shop, and range situated on 15 acres. The academy is privately owned and operates on a schedule of 2,040 instructional hours, requiring about 13 months for completion. Housing must be obtained in the vicinity. Upon graduation a certificate is awarded.

**Colorado School of Trade.** (1575 Hoyt St., Lakewood, CO 80215.) Lakewood is in the Denver Metro area, and housing must be obtained in the vicinity. This privately owned school was founded in 1947, and operates a gun shop where the students repair firearms brought in by customers. The program consists of 1,800 instructional hours, and requires 14 months to complete. Upon completion, an Associate Occupational degree is awarded.

**Trinidad State Junior College.** (600 Prospect St., Trinidad, CO 81082.) Trinidad is located in southern Colorado near the New Mexico border. The campus is 17 acres and has on-campus living. The school operates on a two-semester year, and awards an Associate degree in gunsmithing requiring two years of study. Also offered is an advanced-study course in gun repair after completion of the degree.

## Iowa

**Southeastern Community College.** (1015 South Gear Ave., West Burlington, IA 52655.) Located in the southeastern tip of Iowa, Southeastern Community College has on-campus housing on its 160 acres. The college operates on a two-semester year, and offers both certificate and degree programs. Three semesters totaling 49 credits (740 hours) are required for the certificate, while five semesters and 18 additional gunsmith credits (1028 hours) with 18 educational credits (288 hours) are required for the degree program. Total time is approximately 1 1/2 years for a certificate and 2 years for the degree.

## Minnesota

**Pine Technical College.** (1000 Fourth St., Pine City, MN 55063.) Pine City is located on the eastern border of Minnesota, 60 miles north of Minneapolis/St. Paul. The school operates on a three-semester year, and has both certificate and degree programs. The certificate requires 90 credits (990 hours) in gunsmithing, plus 18 credits (198 hours) of general education. The degree program consists of 54 credits (594 hours) of gunsmithing and 54 credits (594 hours) of educational courses. Both require six semesters or two years for completion.

## Missouri

**Professional Gunsmiths of America,** Technical Training Course. (Route 1, Box 224F, Lexington, MO 64067.) This privately owned institution is located in western Missouri about 50 miles east of Kansas City. The school offers an apprenticeship-style program of 1,920 hours or about one year's duration. Students participate in the functioning of an operating gun shop. Housing must be obtained in the vicinity.

## North Carolina

**Montgomery Community College.** (P.O. Box 787, Troy, NC 27371.) The school is located in central North Carolina just south of Asheboro. The 153-acre campus contains a firing range, but does not provide student housing. The college operates on a four-semester year and offers one- and two-year certificate programs. The one-year program consists of 58 credits (990 hours) of gunsmith instructions and 6 credits (54 hours) of educational studies. The full 2-year program requires 46 additional credits (1,125 hours) of gunsmithing classes. Montgomery also offers a one-year metal-engraving curriculum for those who fancy the more artistic side of gunsmithing.

**Piedmont Community College.** (P.O. Box 1197, Roxboro, NC 27573.) Roxboro, in the north-central part of the state, is close to the Virginia border. Piedmont operates on a four-semester year and provides a degree program of 96 units (960 hours) of gunsmith courses and 7 units (70 hours) of educational studies. Time required for completion is two years; housing must be obtained in the vicinity.

## Oklahoma

**Murray State College.** (1 Murray Campus, Tishomingo, OK 73460.) Located in south-central Oklahoma about 100 miles north of Dallas/ Ft. Worth, Texas, and about the same distance south of Oklahoma City, Murray State College offers on-campus living and both certificate and degree programs. The school operates on a two-semester year with either program requiring two years for completion. Both have 57 credits of gunsmithing (855 hours); however, the degree program includes 16 additional credits (240 hours) of educational courses.

## Pennsylvania

**Pennsylvania Gunsmith School.** (812 Ohio River Boulevard, Avalon, PA 15202.) Avalon is a suburb of Pittsburgh, Pennsylvania, located in the western part of the state near the Ohio border. This privately owned school operates on an hourly schedule of 2,500 instructional hours, with 16 months required for completion. Housing must be obtained in the vicinity.

## At Home

**American Gunsmithing Institute.** (P.O. Box 2626, Greenwich, CT 06836-2626.) The institute produces an extensive gunsmithing course that encompasses 56 videotapes, or 103 hours of instruction. Taught by Robert Dunlap, senior instructor at Lassen College's world-renowned school of gunsmithing, the course covers all major brands and action types of handguns, rifles, and shotguns. If you can't or don't want to travel to gunsmithing school, you can still get in-depth gun-working knowledge from the AGI videotape series. ★

# Index

# Index

# Notes

# Notes